Map from Goode's World Atlas
© 1994 by Rand McNally, R.L. 94-S-10

Enchantment of the World

GUYANA

By Marlene Targ Brill

16192

Consultant for Guyana: George I. Blanksten, Ph.D., Professor Emeritus of Political Science, Northwestern University, Evanston, Illinois

Consultant for Reading: Robert L. Hillerich, Ph.D., Professor Emeritus, Bowling Green State University, Bowling Green, Ohio; Consultant, Pinellas County Schools, Florida

CHILDRENS PRESS®

CHICAGO

Music is an important part of Guyanese celebrations.

Project Editor: Mary Reidy
Design: Margrit Fiddle

Library of Congress Cataloging-in-Publication Data

Brill, Marlene Targ.
   Guyana / by Marlene Targ Brill.
      p.   cm. – (Enchantment of the world)
   Includes index.
   Summary: Discusses the geography, history, economics,
government, people, and culture of this South American
country.
   ISBN 0-516-02626-7
   1. Guyana–Juvenile literature. [1. Guyana.]
I. Title. II. Series.
F2368.5.B75   1994
988.1–dc20   94-7007
                                                    CIP
                                                    AC

Picture Acknowledgments
AP/Wide World Photos: 48 (left), 54, 55
The Bettmann Archive: 30 (left), 31
D. Donne Bryant Stock: © **Nancy Q. Kirk,** 12 (bottom), 66,
78; © **Vince DeWitt,** 62, 65, 69, 74 (top), 83 (left), 85 (left),
89 (left), 103; © **J. Nations,** 97 (left)

© **Carol Lee,** Cover, 4, 18 (2 photos), 19, 22 (top & bottom
right), 43, 60, 67, 71, 72, 74 (bottom left), 85 (right), 86
(2 photos), 87, 88, 90 (2 photos), 94, 95 (inset), 96 (left), 98
(bottom), 105, 122
Embassy of The Republic of Guyana: 10
North Wind Picture Archives: 29, 30 (right), 32 (2 photos),
34, 37
Chip and Rosa Maria de la Cueva Peterson: 6, 14, 17, 33,
38, 63, 64, 74 (bottom right), 77 (right), 81 (2 photos), 83
(right), 84, 92 (2 photos), 98
Photri: 26, 93
Reuters/Bettmann: 89 (right)
Root Resources: © **Gail Nachel,** 23 (left); © **Kenneth W.
Fink,** 24 (top right); © **Doug Perrine,** 25 (top left)
South American Pictures: 28; © **Tony Morrison,** 5, 15, 23
(right), 76 (2 photos), 77 (left); © **Peter Williams,** 59, 95, 96
(right), 97 (right)
Tom Stack & Associates: © **Kevin Schafer,** 24 (bottom
left); © **Warren Garst,** 24 (bottom right); © **P. L. Brock,** 25
(bottom left)
SuperStock International, Inc.: © **Hubertus Kanus,** Cover
Inset, 100
Travel Stock: © **Tony Tedeschl,** 12 (top), 20, 68, 102;
© **Buddy Mays,** 22 (bottom left)
UPI/Bettmann Newsphotos: 9, 47, 48 (right), 50 (2 photos),
52 (2 photos)
Valan: © **Karl Weidmann,** 25 (right)
Len W. Meents: Maps on 91, 100, 102
**Courtesy Flag Research Center, Winchester,
Massachusetts 01890:** Flag on back cover
Cover: Canoeing on a jungle creek
Cover Inset: Georgetown

Thatch homes of the Warrau tribe on the Orinoco River Delta

TABLE OF CONTENTS

Chapter 1 *One People, One Nation, One Destiny* (An Introduction). 7

Chapter 2 *Land of Many Waters* (Geography, Vegetation, Animal Life). 13

Chapter 3 *From Villages to Colonies* (Prehistory to the Early Nineteenth Century). 27

Chapter 4 *Many Faces of Guyana* (Nineteenth and Twentieth Century History). 39

Chapter 5 *Emerging Guyana* (Independence, Government, Foreign Relations). 51

Chapter 6 *A Look into the Future* (Natural Resources, the Economy, Transportation, Communication). 61

Chapter 7 *Land of Six Peoples* (People and Their Traditions). 75

Chapter 8 *A Trip Along the Waterways* (A Tour). 91

Mini-Facts at a Glance. 108

Index. 123

Fields of sugarcane surround these homes southwest of Georgetown.

Chapter 1

ONE PEOPLE, ONE NATION, ONE DESTINY

"One People, One Nation, One Destiny," is the slogan on Guyana's national emblem. The motto represents the country's hope of uniting its many races and regions. For the present, Guyana inches toward that goal. The country's past, however, reveals another story. Guyana's history is a tale of great struggles to find a single national voice.

Guyana is located just north of the equator on the northeastern coast of South America. For centuries, Guyana was ruled by European countries. First the Dutch, then the British invaded the awesome rain forests inhabited by Amerindians, Guyana's earliest people. Legends about a famed city of gold lured Europe's explorers to northeast South America. Once there, settlers established colonies along Guyana's fertile shores. Sugarcane became Guyana's gold, as large plantations sprang up on the coast.

To farm vast tracts of land, Europeans imported Africans as slaves. Slavery fueled Guyana's economy until 1807, when Britain ordered an end to slave trade. Landowners searched for other laborers to work the land cheaply. Boatloads of Portuguese, Chinese, and East Indians contracted to replace the slaves in exchange for transportation, a skimpy roof over their head, and poor wages. Each ethnic group–Amerindian, European, African, East Indian, Chinese, and people of mixed background–brought its own culture, a culture that longed to be treated fairly. Slave rebellions, strikes, and uprisings erupted regularly.

Great Britain ran Guyana as a colony for more than 150 years. Georgetown, the capital, developed a quiet elegance much like its parent country. A limited education system and scattered settlements sprouted along the coast and inland on major rivers that separated land areas. Sporadic explorations inland for gold, diamonds, and the mineral bauxite pushed the native Amerindians farther into Guyana's natural wonderland.

After independence in 1966, Guyana became divided by race. By then, East Indians and Africans accounted for the largest segments of Guyana's population. While these groups vied for power, Europeans and Amerindians pressed to get their share. Conflict continued.

In 1970 the country became the Cooperative Republic of Guyana with a form of government that promised unity and advancement. But the racial divisions were too great. Pains from being silenced for so long by British control were too hurtful. It took another fifteen years before Guyana could even begin to value its cultural diversity.

The early 1990s brought a strong sense of national spirit. New government fostered feelings of unity through state and ethnic

Schoolchildren gathered to rehearse the new national anthem during independence celebrations in 1966.

celebrations. Guyanese welcomed leaders of varied races into government. But the economy remained weak and the people poor. Georgetown and other villages lost their glow from colonial days and had little money to restore the luster. The challenge to build a single nation from Guyana's divided past continued. Yet, the Guyanese people looked forward to a time when they would be one people with a single destiny.

FLAG, ANTHEM, AND EMBLEM

Guyanese glorify their cultural unity in their symbols. The national anthem sung at public events trumpets the striking unspoiled beauty of the land. But it also sings the praises of Guyana's varied cultural heritage.

> Great land of Guyana, diverse though our strains
> We are born of their sacrifice and heirs of their pains
> And ours is the glory, their eyes did not see
> One land of six people, united and free.

Guyana's coat of arms

Guyana's national coat of arms is described in the paragraph below. The designs were suggested by three Guyanese artists and adapted by the Royal College of Arms in England. The streamer below the coat of arms bears the national motto: One People, One Nation, One Destiny.

Guyana's national emblem indicates more than a motto. The coat of arms shows the value placed on natural resources as the hope for Guyana's economic future. A hoatzin, Guyana's national bird, decorates the shield center. To the right and left of the shield are two jaguars. One holds a pickax that stands for Guyana's valuable bauxite mining. The other grasps a cane representing the importance of sugarcane farming. A diamond in the Indian headdress above the shield illustrates gemstone mining. Guyana remains committed to its agricultural and mining roots.

Guyana's flag is different from any other national banner. The bright green background symbolizes the country's rich forests and agriculture. A golden arrow outlined in white cuts through the background. The gold stands for the wealth of minerals hidden within the earth, and the white represents the nation's many waters. The left edge of the flag shows a brilliant red triangle. The red characterizes the people's fiery spirit. Black edging on the triangle's two inner sides reflects the courage and strength that Guyanese need to propel the golden arrow into a bright future.

HOLIDAYS AND CELEBRATIONS

Guyana highlights cultural diversity through its many festivals. There are thirteen national holidays, many specific to one ethnic group but shared by all. Muslims celebrate Youman Nabi to honor their holy prophet Muhammad's birthday in January. In November Hindus rejoice on Deepavali, the festival of lights. Chinese light firecrackers and perform a dragon dance to celebrate the beginning of the lunar year on the first new moon after January 26. And Christians honor the birth and death of Christ on Christmas and Easter. These feast days add to the spirit of Guyana.

The one celebration that applauds all groups is Mashramani, or Mash. This marks the birth of the republic. The official date is February 23. But Guyanese often celebrate the entire month.

The word "Mashramani" is an Amerindian term. It is a name for any celebration held after completion of a group project. The term fits the anniversary of the cooperative republic because Mashramani brings people together.

A flag-raising ceremony the night of February 22 opens the celebration. Parades, floats, colorful displays, game competitions, and music follow. The festivities allow each ethnic group to express itself. The Guyanese call their lively expressions "jumping up." By recognizing every group's place in history, Guyana supports its faith in its national goal: to mold one people with a united future.

*Roaring Orinduik Falls (above) and a gently flowing section of
the Mazaruni River (below) in Guyana, the land of many waters*

Chapter 2

LAND OF MANY WATERS

For centuries, writers and painters have celebrated Guyana's striking landforms and wildlife. Great variety and dazzling charm have lured nature lovers to the country. Sandy plains, rocky mountains, tropical forests, and dry grasslands bear untold natural resources and untamed beauty.

Guyana's most noted resources are waterways. Amerindians named the area *Guyana*, meaning "land of many waters." The name derived from the teeming waterways that snaked through the country, providing transportation and livelihood to these early inhabitants. European explorers adopted the name. They used it to define the entire area that is present-day Guyana, Suriname, French Guiana, and parts of Brazil and Venezuela. English adventurers referred to their New World colony as "Guiana."

Modern Guyana occupies about 10 percent of the original Guiana region. The country covers 83,000 square miles (214,969 square kilometers) on the northeast rim of South America. Its size is slightly smaller than the state of Idaho in the United States.

Guyana's 270-mile (435-kilometer) coastline faces the Atlantic Ocean to the northeast. Brazil borders to the south and southwest. Venezuela lies to the northwest and Suriname is to the east. These two countries maintain long-standing boundary disputes with Guyana.

The Dutch built floodgates and seawalls similar to the ones in Holland.

THE COASTAL PLAIN

Guyana has four distinct physical regions: coastal plain, hilly sand and clay belt, interior savannas, and highlands. The coastal plain is the smallest yet most densely populated region. A narrow strip of plain runs from Suriname to the Venezuelan border, and is 2 to 30 miles (3.2 to 48 kilometers) wide. The northwestern portion has infertile soil, however. So 90 percent of the people and almost all of the country's agricultural products come from the remaining 180-mile (290-kilometer) stretch of land to the east.

Much of the coastal plain lies below sea level at high tide. To farm the land, the first Dutch settlers built a system of drainage canals, seawalls, and dikes. Today, 140 miles (225 kilometers) of seawall extend along the ocean to hold water back from crops and homes. For the first mile inland, farmers cultivate pasture grasses and rice, products that withstand flooding.

An aerial view of the Essequibo River

The rich coastal soil has resulted from many years of erosion. The rivers of Guyana race northward toward the Atlantic Ocean. The strong current carries *alluvium*, small particles of soil from the land. Over time, tons of alluvial soil reach the ocean off the coast.

RIVERS AND TRANSPORT

Four main rivers empty into the Atlantic on the northeast coast. The Courantyne, Berbice, Demerara, and Essequibo rivers have many branches that cut into the coastal plain and hinder land transportation. The Essequibo, the longest and widest of the four rivers, and the Courantyne originate to the south in Brazil. The Courantyne River shaped Guyana's eastern border with Suriname.

Although Guyana has miles of waterways, only a fraction are navigable. Strong currents, rapids, sandbars, and mud flats pose hazards to water travel. Poor drainage from the mountains and grasslands contributes to flooding and formation of swamps. During high tide, travel inland from the coastal plain is limited.

Boat travel on the Courantyne and Demerara rivers is possible for only 60 miles (97 kilometers), and boats on the Essequibo can travel for 40 miles (64 kilometers). The Berbice River is accessible for 100 (161) of its 370 miles (595 kilometers).

HILLY SAND AND CLAY BELT

About 40 miles (64 kilometers) inland from the coast is a wide span (from 80 to 100 miles; 129 to 161 kilometers) of rolling hills. The hills are unusual for their white sand and clay soil covered with dense tropical forests. These sandy hills rise from 50 feet (15 meters) near the coastal plain to 400 feet (122 meters) inland. They form the largest region in Guyana, covering about 85 percent of the country.

Most of Guyana's natural resources come from the tropical forest. Bauxite, the ore used to make aluminum, is mined from the white sands. Manganese is dug from the plateau at Arakaka on the Barima River in the far northwest. Scattered gold, diamonds, and other minerals provide small but valuable deposits to bolster Guyana's economy. Hardwood lumber represents another great resource. The forest contains about one thousand different varieties of trees. Some timber, like the greenheart tree, is valuable for construction. Other wooded areas near waterways are being explored for hydroelectric power.

THE HIGHLANDS

The Guyana Highlands combine with the Brazilian Highlands to form the oldest geological formations in South America. Some archaeologists claim the crystal rocks are 600 million years old.

An Amerindian village

Through the years, wind, water, and temperature changes eroded the soil and clay. The erosion created magnificent waterfalls and left deposits of gold and diamonds.

The oldest mountain range is the Kanuku Mountains near Guyana's southeastern border with Brazil. Ancient rock crystals and rock engravings go back to pre-Columbian cultures. Today, the area is home to many Amerindians who remained in the region after colonization. Most still live as their ancestors, planting root crops and fishing. Transportation into the highlands is hazardous, so Amerindians generally go about their business with little contact with modern cultures.

Top: The Kaieteur Falls are a magnificent sight.
Above: The Potaro River flows through the bottom of Kaieteur Gorge.

The Pakaraima Mountain range is in the distance.

Guyana's highlands produce many spectacular waterfalls. The most forceful is Kaieteur Falls on the Potaro River. Kaieteur Falls has the seventh greatest flow and is one of the highest single-drop waterfalls in the world. It sends more than 23,400 cubic feet (175,500 gallons or 664,338 liters) of water per second over the rim to a straight drop of 741 feet (226 meters). According to Amerindian legend, the Kaieteur was named after Kai, a great chief of the Patamona tribe. Kai sacrificed his life to the Great Spirit, Makonaima, by going over the falls in a canoe. The beloved chief wanted Makonaima to save his tribe from a rival Carib tribe.

Two other major waterfalls send less forceful torrents of water from higher ridges. Swift-flowing waters from King George VI Falls plunge 1,600 feet (488 meters) along the Utashi River. Great Falls drops 840 feet (256 meters) on the Mazaruni River.

The highest peak in Guyana is Mount Roraima, which reaches 9,094 feet (2,772 meters). Mount Roraima is located in the Pakaraima Mountain range on the western frontier where Guyana, Venezuela, and Brazil meet. The Pakaraima Mountain Range includes the largest of many flat-topped peaks in the highlands.

Rupununi Savanna

SAVANNAS

Two separate dry, grassy plains, called savannas, make up about 10 percent of Guyana. Many rivers run through each. Spotty clumps of savanna grass provide pasture for the farms that operate in these regions.

The smaller savanna lies about 60 miles (97 kilometers) inland from the northeast coast. A white sandy forested area encloses the savanna's almost 2,000 square miles (5,180 square kilometers). The larger Rupununi Savanna is a plateau that rises about 250 feet (76 meters) above sea level. The east-west Kanuku Mountains cut through the Rupununi and divide it into northern and southern sections.

WEATHER

Guyana has a tropical climate. Hot, rainy weather continues year-round throughout the country. Inland temperatures range from 66 to 103 degrees Fahrenheit (18.8 to 39.4 degrees Celsius). Steady northeast sea breezes along the coast temper the constant heat and high humidity. Coastal temperatures vary from 74 to 86 degrees Fahrenheit (23.3 to 30 degrees Celsius).

Although Guyana experiences heavy rainfall, the country encounters few of the tornadoes, hurricanes, or earthquakes that plague nearby countries. Rainy seasons run from May to August and from November to January. Rainfall is greatest along the coast and in the highlands. Coastal rains reach an annual average of 90 inches (229 centimeters). An average of 60 inches (152 centimeters) falls on the interior savanna.

As in most countries, varying rainfall affects farm production. Guyana farmers harvest sugarcane and rice during the dry season between September and November. Dry seasons can be incredibly dry, whereas rainy seasons bring torrents of rain that cause extreme flooding. If rains are heavy, production and the ability to harvest crops suffer. Severe drought also causes crop loss and forest fires.

PLANT LIFE

Heavy rainfall and varying landforms contribute to Guyana's diverse vegetation. Saltwater grasses along the coast nourish marshes and mangrove swamps. The savanna, however, has poorer soil. The area grows clusters of grass and scattered palm trees. Interior tropical rain forests produce most of the country's varied vegetation. Greenheart and wallaba trees from the north and mora lumber from sandy soils are practically indestructible.

The rain forest (above) is filled with animals, birds, and exotic flowers. Some of the flowers are torch ginger (below) and heliconia (right).

Epiphytes *(left) growing in the rain forest, and*
enormous lily pads (right) in a creek in the Rupununi Savanna

Therefore, they are the basis of Guyana's construction industry.
Furniture is made from such hardwoods as siruaballi, hubaballi,
and balata.

Rain forests encourage growth of a variety of *epiphytes*, which
are plants that grow on other plants but rely on air and water for
nutrients. The beauty of orchids, Spanish moss, and pineapple
epiphyte plants is beyond description.

Unusual flowering plants grow throughout Guyana. The most
famous is the Victoria Regia lily. This water lily is found in still
ponds. Lily leaves grow up to 6 feet (1.8 meters) wide. The
Victoria Regia was discovered by a German-born British explorer
and surveyor, Robert Schomburgk, in 1837. Since that time, it has
become Guyana's national flower.

Some animals found in the tropic areas of Guyana are the three-toed sloth (above left), the naked throated bellbird (top right), and the giant anteater (bottom right).

WILDLIFE

Naturalists maintain that tropic areas like Guyana are home to almost 90 percent of the world's wildlife. The number and variety of animals that live here are awesome.

The most common animals are monkeys and deer. Sloths hang upside down in trees, and anteaters, armadillos, and tapir roam the rain forests. Caymans, turtles, and reptiles share swamps and rivers with exotic arapaimas, electric eels, and game fish like lukanani, haimara, pacu, and biara. Sharks and stingrays live

Both the manatees (top left) and peccaries (left), once hunted for meat, are now protected. The rarest, and national, bird is the hoatzin (above).

offshore with the more common snappers and groupers. The manatee, the large mammal that was once hunted for meat, hides, and blubber oil, now enjoys protective status as an endangered species. Small wild pigs called peccaries also have been overused for food.

Birds are as varied as other life forms in Guyana. Colorful birds range from the familiar hummingbird, vulture, and kingfisher to the greenheart, tinamou, and bellbird. The rarest bird is the hoatzin. This creature is found chiefly in Guyana and is the national bird. So many rare creatures exist in Guyana that conservationists have traveled here for decades to study nature.

Prehistoric rock paintings have been found on cliffs along the Mazaruni River.

Chapter 3

FROM VILLAGES
TO COLONIES

AMERINDIANS

Little is known about Guyana's first inhabitants, the
Amerindians. Archaeologists believe they descended from Stone
Age Asians who followed their food supply across the land
bridge that existed during the Ice Age between Siberia and Alaska
and continued southward. Eventually, groups settled throughout
North and South America.

Stories about these people passed by word of mouth; there was
no written language. Therefore, researchers are still uncovering
details about Amerindian early origins and lifestyles.

Amerindian was the collective name given to northern South
American Indians. Most coastal Amerindians originated from one
of three main nations that spoke either Arawak, Carib, or Warrau.
They lived in scattered villages along Guyana's many waterways
and constructed homes of wooden poles and cane and rattan
plants. The shape of Amerindian homes varied with the tribe and

*A drawing shows Caribs making cassava
bread (left) and crushing sugarcane (right).*

importance of the people who lived inside. The Warrau built
thatch homes on stilts along the swampy beaches of the Orinoco
River Delta in present-day Venezuela and parts of Guyana.
Nearby in northern Guyana, the peaceful Arawak lived in fixed
villages of round homes in northern Guyana. They moved farther
north onto the Caribbean islands when the fierce Caribs chased
them from the rain forests. Arawak claimed that Caribs raided
villages, killed men, and carried away the women. As European
explorers landed on South American shores, they heard that
Caribs ate human flesh. The name cannibal originated from the
Arawak description of Carib tribespeople. Researchers still
question the truth of these reports.

Amerindians were expert boat handlers. They traveled in canoes
sculpted from hollowed tree trunks. Some boats held more than
fifty travelers. Large canoes served as warships and as
transportation for moving entire villages to new locations.

Amerindians fished, farmed, and hunted. Arawak tribes applied
the most advanced methods. Farmers dug fields with irrigation

Today bows and arrows are still used by Amerindians for catching fish.

ditches and fertilized crops with wood ash, urine, and plant wastes. They planted manioc, potatoes, beans, and peanuts. Bitter roots of the manioc plant formed the basis of a soup, called pepper pot, that was boiled in large kettles over open fires. Starch from manioc roots is still used to prepare tapioca pudding.

The Arawak fished with spears or hooks and lines. They carved stone and wood into simple tools for hunting and cooking and into furniture. They wove nets from cotton and strung them from walls for sleeping, introducing Europeans to hammocks.

EUROPEANS ARRIVE

Christopher Columbus is thought to have been the first European explorer to sight Guyana's present coastline on his third voyage to the New World in 1498. Shoreline mud flats and sandbars made navigation dangerous. The overgrown swamps looked unattractive for settlement. Columbus continued his travels until reaching what is now Venezuela before landing. He named

Christopher Columbus (left) and Alonso de Ojeda (right)

the area Guiana. The region included present-day Guyana, Suriname, French Guiana, and parts of Brazil and Venezuela.

A year later Alonso de Ojeda, one of Columbus's mapmakers, returned to Guiana's coast and went ashore. He found dense, bug-infested mangrove swamps and little reason to explore for riches or land suitable for farming. Adventurers from different countries passed Guiana's shores as well. Guiana appeared to have none of the gold or silver that attracted Europeans to other parts of the continent.

Northeastern South America remained unsettled by Europeans during the sixteenth century. Spain sent an expedition under Pedro de Acosta in 1530. On reaching the mouth of the Barima River, the crew was slaughtered by Amerindians. Distrustful natives knew how Europeans had enslaved tribespeople farther south and on the Caribbean islands. Thirty years later, Dutch explorers made the first friendly contact with Guiana's Amerindians. Merchants were so encouraged they built trading

Sir Walter Raleigh

posts. But these were raided, too. The only Europeans willing to brave Guiana's hardships were pirates and convicts.

Interest in northern South America awakened between 1595 and 1616. Sir Walter Raleigh, an English explorer, commanded three trips in search of El Dorado, a great city of gold. Native legends had spread to Europe about a chief of El Dorado who covered himself with gold dust during ceremonies. Some stories told of an entire town of gold wearers and temples filled with yellow rock statues.

Raleigh believed these fantastic stories, even though his crew failed to find El Dorado. After the first disappointing trip, Raleigh wrote *The Discoverie of the large and bewtiful Empire of Guiana* (1596), a blend of legends from natives and earlier explorers. In this book, Raleigh told of the region's amazing wealth and beauty. Although he never found gold, Raleigh's voyages provided the first detailed account of Guiana's coastline and physical features.

On Raleigh's last journey to Guiana, he became sick and his son was killed. Raleigh returned to England without locating the

Ships used by the Dutch (left) and a Dutch West India Company office (right)

fabled city of gold. The angry King James ordered Raleigh's execution. Even though Raleigh failed, much of Europe believed El Dorado existed in unexplored South America. Spain, Holland, Portugal, and France sent many fruitless expeditions.

DUTCH COLONIES

Dutch and English settlers built the first permanent settlement in 1616. The fort was on an island about 40 miles (64 kilometers) from the mouth of the Essequibo River where the Mazaruni and Cuyuni rivers meet. Settlers called the colony *Kijk-orver-al*, meaning "overlooking all," for its safe lookout location. The fort was to be a trading post and eventually farmland for tropical crops. By 1621 the Dutch West India Company controlled the colony. Other settlements emerged along each of the three main rivers–Essequibo, Demerara, and Berbice.

At first, Amerindians welcomed the Europeans as trading partners. Amerindians exchanged dyes, hemp, and woods for European cloth and other goods. Europeans encouraged the

A canal with a closed floodgate

friendly relations. They understood that Amerindians were necessary allies to ensure both trade profits and the safety of the settlements.

The Dutch gradually claimed more land inland to farm tobacco, cotton, and coffee. Guiana never became a large supplier of European crops, however. The inland soil proved to be of poor quality. Southern North American colonies flooded Europe with better, cheaper tobacco and cotton. Gradually, Guiana planters switched to sugarcane, a good crop for fertile coast soil and one unsuitable to the rival North American farms.

The main problem was that coastal farms flooded at high tide. To farm poorly drained land, the Dutch constructed a complex system of dikes and floodgates similar to the ones already in Holland. Canals carried fresh water for irrigation. They enabled boats to haul crops to storage and processing.

*People were captured in Africa, bound, and
marched under guard to be sold as slaves.*

Reclaiming the land from the sea, or *poldering*, costs money.
Wealthy Dutch were the only settlers who could afford the
investment. A select group of men soon owned fewer and larger
plantations.

Considerable labor was needed to develop and work large
sugarcane fields. At first, owners tried to enslave Amerindians,
but these attempts proved unsuccessful. The Dutch turned to the
West India Company to import Africans as cheap labor. By 1770
the company had enslaved more than 15,000 Africans to work in
the Demerara sugar region of Guiana. As demand for workers
grew, English planters started their own business to smuggle
slaves. Within thirty years, the slave population soared to 100,000,
often outnumbering the Dutch and English settlers in some
colonies.

BERBICE SLAVE REBELLION

Slaves suffered horribly. Supervisors called overseers mistreated,
overworked, and degraded men, women, and children. Owners

bought and sold slaves like animals. Families were separated. Most spoke different African languages, so they couldn't speak to each other. The African slaves were stripped of their native language and culture and forced to accept European customs. Any attempts to rebel or escape led to stricter controls. Frightened plantation owners contracted with Amerindians to capture and return runaway slaves.

On February 23, 1763, a house slave named Cuffy organized a revolt at the Magdalenenburg Plantation in the Berbice colony. Africans united to demand better treatment. As the revolt grew stronger, they pressed for an end to slavery. Africans killed thousands of overseers and owners, seized weapons, and forced owners off their plantations. Within a short time, Africans controlled the Berbice colony.

The siege lasted for nearly a year. Berbice's Governor van Hoogenheim eventually silenced the revolt with an army. Infighting among slave groups and reduced supplies helped him defeat the Africans. But Cuffy and two other African leaders, Akara and Accabre, became legends. A sculpture by Philip A. Moore stands in Georgetown, the capital, as a monument to the cause of freedom and the brave Africans who died during the Berbice Slave Rebellion.

BRITISH TAKEOVER

Dutch sugar operations centered along the coastal strip. In 1738 the West India Company appointed a new secretary, Laurens Storm van Gravesande, who made important changes to expand the region. Storm quickly rose from secretary to commander, the colony's highest office. As commander for thirty years, he extended Dutch authority to include Essequibo and Demerara and opened these colonies to foreign settlement. Berbice remained independent.

To encourage English settlement, Storm offered new settlers ten years without paying taxes. Each new colonist received 250 acres (101 hectares) of land facing the sea. Once the original land was cleared, farmers could expand inward 10 miles (16 kilometers). With this plan, the coast developed into long thin strips of sugar estates stretching inland from the water. English planters from the West Indies found Guiana's fertile soil and high sugar profits inviting. They migrated to the Demerara region in droves. Their numbers weakened Dutch control of the colony.

European struggles abroad for trade and land shook Guiana. Spain, France, England, and the Dutch battled for power at home and in the colonies, including those on the South American coast. English plantation owners already objected to higher and higher taxes levied by the West India Company. When French troops occupied Holland in 1781, Britain seized the chance to take Berbice, Essequibo, and Demerara from the Dutch.

For the next thirty-three years Guiana's government changed hands with amazing frequency. The French and Dutch and British fought each other on European soil and in their colonies. During French control of Guiana, the government moved to a new capital called Longchamps. This was a more strategic location, where the Demerara River opens into the Atlantic Ocean. When the Dutch took over, they renamed the site Stabroek.

By 1814, the European powers agreed to settle their differences. Conflict over the Guianas ended. Its current boundaries were established. According to the Treaty of Paris and Congress of Vienna, present-day Suriname went to the Dutch and France established French Guiana.

An 1880 drawing of a bustling Georgetown

Britain gained the strongest foothold in the original Guiana territory. The British government purchased Essequibo, Demerara, and Berbice from the Dutch for about $15 million. Guiana became the only British colony on mainland South America. British rule isolated the colony in history, culture, and economy from all its neighbors.

To win colonists' loyalty, Britain allowed the government to proceed much the same as under the Dutch. A Court of Policy and Combined Court dominated by wealthy sugar planters made most of the decisions in Demerara and Essequibo colonies. The colony of Berbice continued to run its own affairs. By 1831 the government had become unmanageable. Britain reorganized all three territories into British Guiana. The capital, Stabroek, was renamed Georgetown after the British King George III.

The early years under British rule led to major advances. Governor Benjamin D'Urban, British Guiana's first governor, developed Georgetown as a leading coastal city. He constructed schools and libraries. He laid roads and built bridges and railroads. He built Georgetown into a business center.

Poldering projects resumed to reclaim more shoreline for farming. With increased farmland, the sugar industry exploded. Production of coffee and other tropical crops declined as sugar output tripled during the first quarter of the nineteenth century. Britain established British Guiana as a major sugar exporter.

A field of sugarcane with the sugar mill in the distance

Chapter 4

MANY FACES OF GUYANA

Sugar production became the main economic activity of British Guiana throughout the nineteenth century. The demands of growing sugarcane influenced every aspect of life. Eventually, sugarcane farming prompted the unusual ethnic mix that became the heart of modern Guyana. Only Amerindians escaped the sugar industry by retreating farther into the rain forest.

FREEDOM FROM SLAVERY

Unlike Guiana, the British economy was changing. Great Britain entered the Industrial Revolution. Production of goods at home was more profitable than relying on products from the colonies. Free trade and free labor were important to the world economy. Britain saw no reason to continue slavery or special treatment for wealthy colonial planters.

In 1807 British Parliament ended the slave trade. Planters could keep the slaves they owned but could not buy new ones. Fear gripped the plantation owners in British Guiana. They wondered where they would find cheap field-workers. To solve this problem, the owners forced the slaves to have more children.

Colonial slaves, however, assumed the new ruling meant they were free. Revolts broke out when the colonial government denied their freedom. In 1823 more than two hundred slaves died in the East Coast Insurrection, one of the most deadly battles against slavery.

Ten years later, Parliament voted to end slavery throughout the colonies. As of August 1, 1834, former slaves were free but expected to remain on plantations for four more years. During that time, planters were to feed, clothe, and pay wages for labor. Thereafter, slaves were free to leave or to stay as hired help. In exchange, Great Britain paid planters 50 British pounds (about $250) for each slave they owned. This apprenticeship system was a plan to gradually help former slaves and shocked planters adjust to new ways of working together.

THE INDENTURE SYSTEM

The plan failed. Greedy planters dreaded the loss of cheap labor. Their response was to work the slaves harder while they had them. Former slaves refused to stay with cruel bosses who treated them unfairly. After emancipation, most former slaves left the plantations.

A critical shortage of workers followed. Over the next four years, agricultural production dropped by 60 percent. Plantations shut down at an alarming rate. By 1849 only 180 of the 230 sugar plantations and 16 of the 174 coffee and tobacco farms survived.

Many freed slaves were determined to own farms. They wanted to vote and hold office like other landowners. Some pooled their money to buy large portions of abandoned plantations. By 1848 about forty-four thousand Africans lived in one hundred free villages, mainly along the Demerara River. But most former slaves lacked the money and skills to rebuild and maintain the land. In the early days of freedom former slaves often turned to plantation work to fund their farms. But they had little success.

Landowners refused to pay higher wages to attract former slaves. Instead, they devised a new apprentice system, called indentured service, as a source of low-wage labor. Under this system landowners imported thousands of workers. Indentured laborers contracted to work for a minimum of five years. Planters provided transportation, food and housing, and a small wage. At the end of the contract, indentured workers could stay in British Guiana or collect their savings and return home.

The initial search for labor brought small waves of immigrants from England, Ireland, Germany, and the British West Indies. Extreme heat and exhausting work caused considerable illness. Those who survived often deserted. Conditions were little better than under slavery, so few workers who stayed reenlisted.

Landowners turned to Portugal, China, and India for larger numbers of contract laborers. By 1860, thirty thousand Portuguese, mainly from the Madeira Islands, and fourteen thousand Chinese arrived in British Guiana. Portuguese and Chinese workers hated the harsh living conditions and low pay. But unlike earlier European workers, these groups stayed in British Guiana after their indenture expired. The Portuguese opened small shops in towns and villages. By the late 1800s the Portuguese owned 173 of Georgetown's 296 shops. The Portuguese also occupied most stores in New Amsterdam, Guiana's second largest city. Chinese workers became the basis of the grocery trade in the growing towns. After the discovery of gold, they dominated the gold industry.

Planters still needed more laborers. The British government created the office of the agent-general for immigration to bring workers from the colony of India. On May 5, 1838, the first 396 East Indian immigrants arrived in Guiana, and many more ships from India followed. The indenture system ended in 1917. By then, almost 240,000 East Indians had been relocated in British Guiana under indenture contracts. Many East Indians stayed in the colony. Unlike groups before them, a greater percentage remained on plantations after their contracts ended.

GROWING DISCONTENT

Large numbers of Africans and indentured workers outnumbered the English plantation owners. Each immigrant group settled into other jobs after plantation life. Yet they failed to loosen the power held by the wealthy planters.

Africans benefited most from the Compulsory Education Act of 1876. They saw education as a way off poor farms and a path to better jobs. By 1900, most of the teachers, skilled tradespeople, and low-level government workers in British Guiana were Africans. These jobs brought a steady flow of Africans to urban areas, where Portuguese and Chinese shopkeepers expanded their operations.

East Indians, including those who left plantations, stayed isolated. Their numbers kept alive the values and customs from home. East Indians practiced either the Hindu or the Muslim religion. Their religion excluded them from Guiana's education system. Christian churches ran the schools and taught religious

East Indians started Guyana's rice farming.

classes, so East Indian parents refused to send their children to
school. Without education, jobs in government and the professions
remained closed.

One avenue open to East Indians was rice farming, a skill
brought from their homeland. Rice required the same climate as
sugar but less investment and land. Many East Indians found they
could save enough money to buy small plots of land for rice
farming. During the early 1900s, almost 50 percent of the East
Indians left sugar plantations for rice farms. Successful rice
farmers bought more land. By 1905, British Guiana produced
enough rice to export. Many East Indians earned enough money
from rice to open small shops. They joined British Guiana's
growing middle class.

Progress by former slaves and indentured workers did little to
increase their political power. In 1850 only 916 men could vote—
out of 130,000 people. By the turn of the century, groups of
merchants, shopkeepers, and professionals demanded a voice in
government. The Combined Court, the ruling body of wealthy

planters, resisted any change. Worker response was to petition Britain's Queen Victoria for representation in British government. In 1891, Britain lowered income qualifications for service on the Combined Court and expanded the colonial governor's power. These changes to reduce control by Britain and Guiana's wealthy were the most sweeping up to that time. By 1915 the number of eligible male voters climbed to 4,312. However, 46 percent of the voters were British landowners, and they accounted for only 1.7 percent of the total population. British Guiana still had a long way to go for equality among all segments of the population.

TRADE UNIONS

British Guiana's economy worsened after the indenture system ended. Sugar planters lost their ability to compete in worldwide markets. Rice production continued to lure East Indian workers from sugar farms. With a growing labor shortage, sugar production dropped. Prices of rice and sugar plummeted after World War I.

In 1917, the first bauxite mines opened along the Demerara River. Companies from Canada and the United States rushed to develop the mines. Prospectors discovered gold and diamonds, attracting explorers farther inland to find riches. Disputes over who owned the mined land gave rise to new groups with special interests. Ethnic differences underscored the competition to gain economic and political influence. Sugar planters ignored the discontent and struggled to keep their advantage over everyone.

Trade unions, organizations of workers in similar industries, allowed the combined voice of many people to be heard. Hubert Critchlow assembled the first union of African dockworkers. He had led earlier strikes that resulted in reducing the workday by one hour. In 1922 his British Guiana Laborer Union protested low wages and long hours without overtime pay. Within a year the union claimed thirteen thousand members.

The growth of unions in British Guiana paralleled their progress in Great Britain. In 1928 the British Parliament ordered its colonies to recognize unions. About the same time, Ayube Edun, a British-educated East Indian, challenged the living and working conditions of Guianese sugar plantation workers. His cause became linked with the concerns of the entire East Indian community. The resulting Man-Power Citizens Association (MPCA) was the first organization representing East Indians. Moreover, the MPCA was the first recognized group to bargain with the Sugar Producers' Association of wealthy landowners. The union's success encouraged workers from other fields to organize.

GROWTH OF POLITICAL PARTIES

Great Britain made meager attempts to allow its colony a greater voice in government. In 1928, Britain abolished the Combined Court and replaced it with a one-house legislature. But the legislature contained only a minority of elected members, and the queen appointed a governor to preside over the court. Government decisions still remained in the hands of the faraway British government with support from local wealthy planters.

Throughout the 1930s British Guiana's economy weakened further. The Great Depression caused lower prices for rice and sugar. High unemployment led to violent demonstrations in many British colonies. The British government appointed Lord Moyne head of a committee to investigate the social and economic problems in British Guiana. The Moyne Commission interviewed four hundred people from 1938 to 1939.

An important outcome of the report was the 1943 constitutional revision. This revision increased the number of elected members in legislatures and allowed political parties. It also established reduced qualifications for voting and holding office, including the right for women to vote. World War II and postwar problems postponed any changes until 1947. That year, British Guiana held its first election since 1935.

The 1947 election opened fourteen positions on the legislature. Most voters were divided between the two major ethnic groups–East Indian, the larger group, and African. One hopeful was Cheddi Jagan, son of an East Indian sugar foreman who criticized the MPCA. He accused sugar union bosses of secretly selling out to plantation owners. Voters listened. At age twenty-nine, Cheddi Jagan became the youngest member of the legislature, representing the sugar estate area of East Demerara.

Jagan and his North American-born wife, Janet Rosenberg Jagan, had returned to British Guiana in 1943 after education in the United States. Cheddi Jagan, who had a degree in dentistry, opened a dental practice on a sugar estate. He heard worker complaints and saw how they were treated by planters and the union. He and Janet sought greater equality among all British Guiana's rich and poor. Equality for the Jagans meant socialism, a form of government that combines human and property resources for everyone to share. Cheddi Jagan wanted improved health standards, voting rights for all adults, and redistribution of excess land owned by sugar planters.

Involvement in sugar strikes offered the Jagans opportunities for greater visibility. In 1948 sugar workers led a peaceful strike for

In 1948 more than seven thousand sugar workers marched in a strike for better wages and working conditions.

better wages and work conditions. The walkout turned violent, however, and five sugar cutters died. In sympathy, the Jagans organized a funeral march from Enmore to Georgetown. The demonstration attracted the attention of African leaders.

Both Jagans realized the importance of formal political groups to create real change for workers. They also understood that African support was critical for any movement to succeed. Cheddi and Janet Jagan joined with an African and Guianese, Forbes Burnham, a lawyer who had studied in England, to form the

Left: A jubilant Cheddi Jagan after the People's Progressive party won elections in 1953. Right: Five months later Jagan, seen here with his wife Janet, was removed from office.

People's Progressive party (PPP). Burnham became party chairperson; Janet Jagan was appointed secretary general; and Clinton Wong, a Chinese-born businessman, was senior vice-chairman. The joint effort succeeded in winning eighteen of the twenty-four seats in the 1953 election.

From the beginning Cheddi Jagan and Burnham disagreed over who was to lead the legislature. They finally agreed that Cheddi Jagan would be prime minister. Burnham accepted the Minister of Education post, and Janet Jagan became the first woman elected to the legislature.

Great Britain and the United States feared Cheddi Jagan's political beliefs were too close to those of the socialist Soviet Union. Less than five months after Cheddi Jagan became prime minister, the British governor declared an emergency. He suspended the constitution and removed Cheddi Jagan from office. Jagan spent six months in jail.

The crisis put further strains on the PPP. Burnham openly opposed Jagan's emphasis on drastic social and economic change. He stressed a more national goal of independence from Britain. In

1955, Burnham officially broke with the PPP. He formed a new party called the People's National Congress (PNC). The split left East Indian voters in Jagan's PPP. African and moderate voters sided with Burnham, who became mayor of Georgetown.

Britain lifted military rule in 1957. Jagan and his party won the election the same year. Jagan claimed to head the party that represented all Guyanese. He pressed for self-government as promised. But racial conflict deepened. Jagan distributed land in a program that favored East Indians. Of the 90,000 acres (36,422 hectares) of reclaimed land, most went to East Indian rice farmers. Jagan ended import controls that previously favored European interests. Between 1957 and 1960, rice production increased twofold.

Jagan won again in the 1961 elections. The People's National Congress obtained almost the same number of votes as the PPP. Yet Burnham's party secured only eleven seats in the legislature compared to the PPP's twenty seats.

After the election, tensions increased at an alarming rate. Burnham's supporters insisted on a new voting system. The United Force, a party of Europeans and Amerindians, sided with Burnham. The United Force worried about East Indian control of government. By now, about 50 percent of the people were East Indian and 30 percent were African.

Over the next three years, violent protests erupted. Rioters destroyed millions of dollars in property and caused many injuries and several deaths. Georgetown was hit hardest. Non-East Indians protested Jagan's policies. When Britain promised election changes, Jagan supporters took to the streets. Poverty fueled the protests. But the question of race overshadowed every aspect of government.

Above: The people carried posters to show the British and the world that they wanted independence.
Left: Colonial Secretary Duncan Sandys

Chapter 5

EMERGING GUYANA

INDEPENDENCE

Great Britain called a constitutional convention in October 1963 to create an independent government. Jagan, Burnham, and Peter d'Aguiar of the Portuguese party traveled to London to find a way to end their conflict and unite the colony for independence. Burnham and d'Aguiar insisted a new voting system be in place before independence. Jagan proposed keeping the current system and holding elections after independence.

Negotiations dragged on. The leaders could not agree. At home, strikes broke out. Rioters supporting one cause or another took to the streets, burning homes and killing. British troops returned. Foreign governments that feared Guiana's Communist leanings watched carefully. Finally, the colony's leaders agreed to let the British government decide.

Colonial Secretary Duncan Sandys issued a report favoring Burnham's proposal. Racial conflict erupted again. Twenty-three weeks of disorder forced fourteen thousand people from their homes and cost almost $14 million.

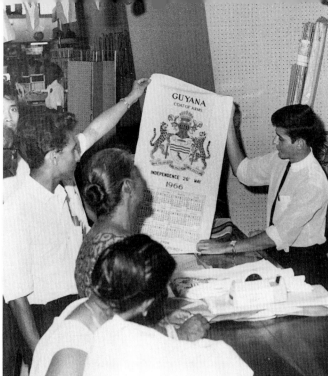

*In 1966 British Guiana became Guyana with Forbes Burnham
(left) as prime minister. A 1966 calendar shows the new
country's coat of arms (right)*

The bitter 1964 election resulted in Jagan's worst fears. The
United Force joined with Burnham to topple Jagan's party. Jagan
challenged the election results and refused to resign. The PPP had
the most votes. But the revised constitution allowed Great Britain
to replace Jagan with Burnham. Two years later, the colony's long
struggle for independence ended. British Guiana became
independent Guyana under Prime Minister Forbes Burnham.

NEW DIRECTIONS

Burnham continued as chief executive until his death in 1985.
Many groups both inside and outside Guyana questioned abuses
in his government. Elections showed how easily one could lose.
So Burnham built strong military support. Future elections
were thought to be fixed. The police restricted the rights of

citizens to meet and have a free press. Yet Burnham maintained control of the divided country. Many of his rulings helped quiet the racial conflict that tore the nation apart. Burnham's early administration promoted new industry, developed secluded rural areas, pressed to ease conditions for farmers, and built roads and bridges.

On February 23, 1970, Burnham converted the government to a republic. The date marked the anniversary of Cuffy's Berbice Slave Rebellion. By 1974 Burnham revised the constitution to give himself more power.

Both changes signaled the start of Guyana as a socialist nation. Downtown Georgetown became the site of the country's first state-run bank. The government took control of the schools. The largest British-owned sugar plantations came under national management. North American and Canadian bauxite interests in Guyana were seized. Within six years, 75 percent of the nation's production of goods and services were government owned and the government controlled most prices. Political loyalty replaced merit and hard work for getting ahead in state-run businesses.

Vice-president Hugh Desmond Hoyte took office after Burnham's death. In December 1985 voters elected Hoyte president for a full term. The People's National Congress retained its hold on government with fixed elections. Hoyte's election seemed to signify business as usual.

TURNABOUT

Hoyte quickly realized he had taken over a failing economy. Burnham's government had led to a reduced quality of life in

President Desmond Hoyte

Guyana. All construction had stopped, and maintenance of
buildings, roads, and schools was neglected. Workers from the
countryside went to live in the city. Large numbers of Guyanese
fled to the United States, Europe, Canada, and other Latin
American countries in search of jobs, education, and training.
Emigration drained Guyana of many educated and skilled
workers. Guyana became the poorest country in South America.

To boost the economy, Hoyte introduced the Economic Recovery
Plan. With this program price controls were lifted, and the
country was opened to mining and oil exploration. For the first
time since Burnham took office in 1964, the government went
outside Guyana for business. Hoyte believed that the flow of
foreign money, experience, and technology was necessary to spark
Guyana's poor economy. He made goodwill trips to Canada,
England, and the United States to broadcast the safety of
Guyanese investments. Guyana joined international organizations.
For the first time, Guyana looked at the tourist industry as a

In 1992 Cheddi Jagan became the new president.

source of income. Travel agents talked about Guyana's diverse population as a reason to visit the country rather than to stay away. By 1991, the economy showed signs of improving.

Even with these changes, the lives of most Guyanese hardly changed. Unemployment and underemployment continued unchecked. Many people remained too poor to buy what they needed to survive. Amerindians were largely ignored.

Discontent led to the rise of Cheddi Jagan as a major power again. Jagan carefully selected an African running mate for the 1992 election. He wanted to shed his image of stressing race in politics. Equally important, he hoped to appeal to more voters.

In 1992 Jagan won the first fair presidential election in decades. Former United States president Jimmy Carter led an international team of observers to supervise elections and the transfer of government.

After elections Jagan pledged an open government. He softened his stand on socialism and promised to continue free trade.

Political enemies welcomed Jagan's decision not to punish them. Instead, Jagan emphasized improvements in health, housing, and education. But he agreed that Guyana must attract new business and be part of the world market to improve its economy.

The new government attracted cautious outside investors and a trickle of returning emigrants. Amerindians participated more in a government open to their interests. Challenges for Guyana's future will be to see Guyana prosper and keep the government free of corruption. Guyanese are beginning to celebrate their ethnic differences rather than exploit them for political gain.

BORDER CONFLICT

Conflict over Guyana's borders goes back to colonial days. In 1835 Britain sent Schomburgk, the explorer and botanist, to mark the Guiana colony's boundaries. His party identified borders that Brazil and Venezuela claimed as theirs.

The dispute went unsettled until gold was discovered in 1880 between the Essequibo and Orinoco rivers. Both Venezuela and Britain asserted rights to all land west of the Essequibo River. The area amounted to about 62 percent of Guiana's territory. A feud began. Britain refused to discuss the problem and broke relations with Venezuela.

Great Britain was a strong power at the time. Venezuela requested help from the United States to settle the problem with Britain. United States President Grover Cleveland agreed. He believed Great Britain's role ran counter to the Monroe Doctrine. The document sought to discourage European countries from meddling in the Western Hemisphere. The British prime minister refused Cleveland's demand to help end the border dispute. The furious Cleveland threatened war. Britain eventually agreed to allow a neutral commission to settle the conflict. The five-member commission of two Venezuelans, two British, and one neutral Russian awarded most of the disputed area to British Guiana.

Land feuds with Venezuela never really ended. Unresolved claims meant Guyana was unable to gain full membership in the Organization of American States (OAS). In 1986 Guyana received nonvoting status in the OAS. The United Nations intervened to help the two countries settle the discord peacefully.

Border differences with Brazil ended in 1905. But another neighbor, Suriname, had made recent land claims that also are being considered by the United Nations. Suriname asserted its rights to all territory east of the New River in southeast Guyana. The area covers about six thousand square miles (about fifteen thousand square kilometers) and is largely uninhabited. Guyana considers its land claims legal against Venezuela and Suriname based on the original report from Schomburgk.

FOREIGN RELATIONS

Independence enabled Guyana to chart its own foreign relations without British involvement. Generally, Guyana's leaders have followed a foreign policy suited to the country's trade and welfare needs. Guyana joined the United Nations in 1966. However, Prime Minister Burnham kept Guyana out of most world affairs and other countries out of Guyana's business. His support was from other nations such as Libya and India, who remained independent of the major powers. Independent countries called their alliance the nonaligned movement.

More recently, Guyana chose to play a role in international

affairs. Guyanese representatives have served on several United Nations committees since 1967. Vice-president General Mohamed Shahabuddeen was elected to the International Court of Justice in 1987. Guyana still allies itself with independent nations but has improved relations with the United States, Russia, Canada, Great Britain, and other Western countries. India and Guyana always have had a special relationship. Guyana's reawakening of pride in ethnic culture brings the two countries closer together.

Guyana's closest ties are with the Caribbean community. Guyana strongly supports economic bonds with these nations. Guyana has been especially active in the Caribbean Free Trade Area (CARIFTA) and the Caribbean Community (CARICOM). These groups foster local and regional growth. They emphasize economic cooperation, coordination of foreign policy, and joint efforts to provide social welfare programs.

GOVERNMENT

Guyana is governed by a fifty-three-member legislature called the National Assembly. Its members are voted into office for five-year terms. Any citizen aged eighteen or older is eligible to vote.

The head of the National Assembly and chief executive is the president. The president is also leader of the majority political party in the legislature. The National Assembly creates laws, but the president has the power to veto them.

Part of the president's duties is to appoint ministers for the legislature and a nine-member cabinet that is responsible to the assembly. The prime minister is next in command and first vice-president of the assembly. The prime minister and cabinet conduct government business.

The High Court Building in Georgetown

The government follows a constitution as the absolute law of the land. The highest court is the Court of Appeal, run by a chancellor. Judges for the Court of Appeal decide civil and criminal cases. Lower, or magistrate, courts hear claims involving small amounts of money. The chancellor and chief justice, who supervise the lower court, are appointed by the president.

Guyana is divided into ten administrative regions. The head of each region presides over a regional democratic council. Local districts are governed by village or city councils.

Overall, Guyana claims to have a democratic government. Its people have constitutional rights to freedom of political opinions regardless of race, ethnic origin, or gender. Government leaders continue to work toward making these rights a reality for all Guyanese.

A display of fresh produce in a market in Georgetown

Chapter 6

A LOOK INTO

THE FUTURE

The early 1990s brought dramatic economic reforms to Guyana. The government moved to cut rising costs and lift many import and export restrictions. The new plan was to attract private local and foreign investors. In turn, business investment would create much-needed jobs and more products.

Unpaid loans to foreign creditors limited rapid economic expansion. Without the flow of credit, Guyana was unable to import products needed for growth. Shortages of spare parts, equipment, and raw materials for agriculture and industry persisted. The average income was about $340 per year, making Guyana the fourth poorest nation in the Western Hemisphere. Recovery plodded along. Still, many segments of the economy showed signs of promise. Agriculture and mining continued to be the most fruitful economic activities. Sugar, rice, and bauxite make up more than 80 percent of Guyana's export profits.

AGRICULTURE

Agriculture accounts for a major part of Guyana's economy, even though only 33 percent of the people and 2 percent of the land are involved in farming. The largest economic boost comes

A wagon hauling bags of rice

from rice production. Rice is essential to local diets and is Guyana's second most important product. Removing government price controls caused rice sales to rise 61 percent in 1992. Up to 2,000 pounds (907 kilograms) of rice per acre grow in the most fertile areas.

Rice farming is a family affair in Guyana. Families own or lease their small, often five-acre (two-hectare), farms from large landowners or the government. They plant before the rainy season in April or May and harvest during the dry season in October. Weed control comes from floodwaters stored in reservoirs. Water flows through a network of irrigation canals and collects in the heavy clay soil, killing the weeds. Most farmers work with hand tools. Water buffalo or oxen haul plows or wagons carrying harvested rice.

Workers on a sugar farm line up to collect their pay.

Sugarcane has always been a major crop in Guyana. Sugar supplies by-products that are key ingredients in rum, molasses, syrups, and medical and industrial alcohols. Dried pulp from sugarcane refining processes is used in making paper products and fuel. Sugar farming and processing employ more workers than any other industry. For years, 100,000 acres (more than 40,000 hectares) of sugar plantations and most of the country's sugar mills have been owned by Guysuco, the national sugar company. Guysuco employs more than twenty-three thousand workers and is the country's largest employer. More recently, Guysuco came under private management. The government continues to support private ownership of sugar lands.

Considerable money and labor are spent fertilizing the soil during dry and wet seasons. Farmers follow a method called flood fallowing to drain and irrigate the land. With fallowing,

Unloading sugarcane at a mill

fields are plowed, then flooded for a minimum of six months. Thereafter, they are drained and planted.

Sugarcane takes from twelve to eighteen months to mature. At harvest, cutters chop the 12-foot (3.7-meter) stalks by hand. The stalks are laid in rows to dry before being transported to mills. Tractors, mules, or oxen pull the cane-filled, flat-bottom barges along Guyana's network of canals to processing plants. Stalk stubbles and roots left in the earth will produce another harvest. However, production drops with each new crop. Farmers repeat flood fallowing and replanting every three or four years to replenish the soil.

Guyana's farmers produce many crops for local use. Food crops consist of cassava, a root made into tapioca; corn; citrus fruits; cocoa, a bean ground into chocolate; coconut; coffee; and vegetables.

In some areas of the Rupununi Savanna and western coastal plain farmers raise livestock, including beef and dairy cattle,

Bauxite processing plant at Linden

goats, sheep, chickens, and pigs. A growing industry for Guyana involves processing ham and bacon.

MINING

Bauxite is Guyana's richest mineral resource and leading export. Considerable bauxite lies beneath the white sand and clay shores of the Demerara River. Once extracted, bauxite is refined into aluminum. Most bauxite mines and processing plants are found at Mackenzie, Demba, and Ituni on the Demerara River and Kwakwani on the Berbice River. The Guyana Mining Enterprise (Guymine), the national mining company, constructed a hydroelectric plant on the Demerara River to furnish power for converting bauxite ore into aluminum. The government has owned the bauxite operations since the 1970s. Recent negotiations, however, authorized private management of Guymine.

For centuries, miners have explored other mineral resources in

Panning for gold is backbreaking work.

Guyana's inland regions. Gold mining proved the most profitable. Companies from the United States, Canada, and Brazil are interested in further gold exploration. A government gold board handles gold sales and export as guided by law. However, most individual miners choose to sell their gold on the open market, where they earn higher prices.

Independent miners called *portnockers* are the heroes of the poor people. They perform backbreaking tasks under the hot sun of the interior. They dig nuggets from the earth and sift through the sediment of the river bottom in search of glistening rock. The dream of every portnocker is to discover a shout, or strike, of gold or diamonds. The possibility of a strike outweighs any threat from fever, hunger, or serious injury. Money from portnocking is so important to Guyana's economy that an Amerindian miner, Ocean Shark, is pictured on the bank ceiling in Georgetown.

The dense tropical forests contain many kinds of valuable timber.

Shark was one of the first Amerindian portnockers. He persisted in his search for gold until he found a shout that made him a wealthy man.

Portnockers have stiff competition from large mining companies. Mining companies comb isolated deposits from the Mazaruni River and other waters of the Pakaraima Mountains. Several mining companies are exploring gold areas in the Essequibo. A large deposit of manganese was located 30 miles (48 kilometers) from the Venezuelan border at Matthews Ridge. Explorers also insist there is oil in the Rupununi Savanna. Government contracts with companies from the United Kingdom, the United States, and Trinidad encourage onshore and offshore oil exploration. Mining and developing these resources is an expensive task.

FORESTS, FISH, AND FACTORIES

Forests hold great economic potential for Guyana. Dense tropical forests with valuable timber cover 75 percent of the land.

Greenheart logs being processed in a lumber mill

Greenheart, a hardwood that resists termites, decay, and moisture, is most in demand. Greenheart logs supply much of Guyana's markets at home and overseas. Most hardwoods and rare trees sold abroad are for manufacture of furniture and decorative woodwork. Within Guyana, forests furnish lumber for construction of homes, bridges, and buildings.

Problems with cutting and transporting logs hamper the growth of forestry into a major industry. The country lacks the facilities to cut, store, and ship logs. Roads are poor or nonexistent through dense forests, and many rivers are impassable. Still, the government wants to expand the timber industry.

Another source of growth is fishing. The government opened the Guyana Fisheries Company in Georgetown. A fishing fleet of shrimp boats joins ocean liners in Georgetown Harbor. Coastal

Shrimp boats and oceangoing vessels dock in Georgetown Harbor.

shrimp and fish from inland streams form the basis of a limited but growing fishing industry.

Guyana's many waterfalls and interior rapids provide great potential for the development of hydroelectric power. Hydroelectric dams could produce energy for homes and manufacturing. Presently, electric power is available mainly along the coast and around major industrial centers on the lower rivers. Main power plants are at Tiger Hill on the Demerara River and inland by Tiboku Falls on the Mazaruni River. Increased hydroelectric power would reduce Guyana's dependence on foreign oil for energy. But building dams takes a great deal of money and technical skill, two resources in short supply.

Without money, energy, and skilled labor to expand,

manufacturing in Guyana is limited. The largest manufacturing business is the Booker Group of companies. Booker is an English firm that began as Booker Sugar Estates more than 170 years ago. Booker operates most of Guyana's sugar plants as well as stores for cars, farm equipment, hardware, electrical goods, office supplies, and medicine. In Georgetown, Booker runs a department store, grocery, and distillery. Booker divisions produce drugs, concrete bricks, livestock feed, and boxes. They process tires and shrimp. Other smaller companies manufacture tobacco products, foodstuffs, soaps, clothing, and jewelry. About 45 percent of Guyana's population work in factories.

TRADING PARTNERS

Guyana must sell goods to other countries. Foreign sales bring the necessary money to fund local projects and increase business. Guyana's closest economic ties are with the United States, the United Kingdom, and the Caribbean Community (CARICOM). Venezuela supplies most of Guyana's oil products. Guyana clearly supports CARICOM's ideas of regional trade. CARICOM's headquarters is in Georgetown, and Guyana funds much of the organization. Guyana also belongs to the International Bauxite Organization and the Latin American and Caribbean Sugar Producers and Exporters Association. Even with these special ties, more exports go to the United Kingdom than import supplies arrive from CARICOM.

Guyana remains a world supplier of bauxite and aluminum, although sales decreased in the 1990s. Other exports include sugar, rice, shrimp, diamonds, molasses, rum, and lumber. Major imports are machinery, vehicles, cloth, footwear, and foods.

Children paddling their canoe

TRANSPORTATION

Guyana's waterways afford the most far-reaching travel. The government built three main ports at Georgetown, New Amsterdam, and Springlands and several smaller harbors. Ferry and steamer services offer transportation along the coast. They carry goods and passengers through canals on sugar estates and into inland navigable rivers. Canoes and motorboats extend travel somewhat farther into forested areas, where Amerindians and the adventurous go.

Guyana has a limited road and highway network. Most paved roads are clustered in the coastal region. One main road stretches 185 miles (298 kilometers) along the coast from Charity on the Pomeroon River to the Courantyne River on the Suriname border. The Harbor Bridge, one of the longest floating bridges in the world (6,074 feet; 1,851 meters), provides two-lane traffic over the Demerara River. There are no bridges at the Essequibo and

Remote areas can be reached easily by airplanes.

Berbice rivers. A few unpaved trails extend into the savanna.
Overcrowded minibuses follow irregular schedules in Georgetown,
and some taxis are available. Some city people travel by bicycle,
unless the roads are flooded.

Guyana's original 60-mile (97-kilometer) railroad is the oldest
railroad in operation outside the United Kingdom. Main coastal
railways connect Georgetown with the Berbice and Essequibo
river regions. Private tracks link bauxite and manganese mines
with rivers or roads.

Air travel connects the coast with remote regions of the country.
Private planes land on shallow rivers and flat land. Guyana
Airways Corporation, the national airline, schedules domestic and
international flights. Local flights take tourists inland to Kaieteur
Falls and the Mazaruni diamond fields. The airline operates out of

the national Timehri International Airport about 26 miles (42 kilometers) from Georgetown. British West Indian Airways and the Dutch airline KLM provide additional flights to Caribbean countries and major European and North American cities.

COMMUNICATION

Under the People's National Congress, the party controlled Guyana's television, radio, and major newspaper. The media performed education services for the government. Since 1985 there has been greater freedom of expression. Pressure from human rights and international groups has opened the doors to varied voices. Catholic and civic groups started small papers with opposing views, although the government has kept its hold on radio and television.

President Jagan encourages access to state-owned print and broadcast media. The single television station remains state-owned for lack of funds to expand. A number of radio stations broadcast different views. Wealthy Guyanese can access satellite stations from abroad. But few other households can afford radios, televisions, or the electricity to run them.

Newspapers play an important role in promoting ideas. *The Guyana Chronicle* is Guyana's daily newspaper. Several weeklies have sprung up since Jagan took office. Most of these are small. The publishers lack the resources for larger publications.

Telegraph service connects Guyana with the United States. Telephones are available throughout the coast and in selected inland settlements. But most workers in remote areas learn about events by word of mouth.

Some of the ethnic groups living in Guyana are African (above),
Amerindian (below left), and East Indian (below right).

Chapter 7

LAND OF SIX PEOPLES

Guyana respects the history and experiences of each ethnic group within its borders. Their combined heritage makes Guyana one of the most fascinating countries in the world.

ONE PEOPLE, MANY ORIGINS

Guyana's population includes six main ethnic groups—Amerindians, East Indians, Africans, Chinese, Europeans (who are mostly Portuguese and English), and people of mixed racial backgrounds. About 90 percent of the 1992 estimated 819,000 citizens live along the coastal plain. The entire population of Guyana averages 10 people per square mile (4 per square kilometer).

Amerindians once were the only people who inhabited Guyana. Today, they make up about 5 percent of the population. The

A young Arawak girl (right) and a Warrau mother and child (far right)

Arawaks, Warraus, Caribs, and Wapisianas are the four major tribes who inhabit tropical forests. The Makusi is the chief group on the savanna.

Amerindians live mostly in secluded areas. Isolated native groups follow traditions from long ago. Men and women wear sandals and simple body cover-ups. Different tribes decorate their bodies with arm and leg bands, jewelry, and paints made from vegetable dyes and animal oils.

Amerindians hunt, farm, raise cattle, and drain a rubberlike sap from the tropical balata tree to sell for industrial products. Traditionally, Amerindians rarely engaged in Guyana's social, political, and economic operations. They moved farther into the forests as development of natural resources threatened their separate lifestyle.

For decades, missionary activities in the interior focused on absorbing Amerindians into Guyanese society. Amerindians

Wapisianas (left) and African-Guyanese (right)

usually greeted missionaries with distrust. The present government chooses to work with Amerindian nations rather than to eliminate them. More recently, larger numbers of Amerindians have migrated to cities and towns. They wear Western clothing and have jobs on cattle farms or in mines or teaching and nursing. Slowly, Amerindians are becoming involved in the government and in helping to make decisions about Guyana's future.

About 40 percent of the Guyanese are of African descent. Africans were kidnapped from their homeland to work as slaves on sugar plantations. Most came from the Guinea coast of West Africa during the seventeenth and eighteenth centuries. Slavery stripped their ancestors of their language and customs. Through the years African-Guyanese adapted to European institutions to survive.

After slavery ended, former slaves settled in small villages.

Guyanese in Georgetown waiting for the ferry to arrive

Because villages offered limited opportunities, many left for jobs in cities or the interior. But close ties with family members living in the villages remain to this day. Some women portnock gold and diamonds. More often women are left with children to cope on their own. Their men go into the rain forest to portnock. African-Guyanese women are very independent.

In cities, Africans participate actively in government, skilled trades, education, and various professions. Those who venture into the interior portnock for gold, mine bauxite, or cut lumber.

Once Africans formed the largest racial group in Guyana. Now more than half the population is of East Indian descent. The East Indian indentured servants who stayed after their work contracts ended remained farmers, either on large sugar estates or independently owned rice farms. East Indians brought their own religions, languages, and dress.

Strong family and cultural bonds continue to support these customs. The head of the household is usually a male. Unlike the women in many African-Guyanese communities, East Indian women have little voice in religion or business outside the household.

Modern East Indians enter fields previously closed to them in government, sales, industry, and trades. Their booths stand next to those of other Guyanese at local markets. They sell gold and other products. Yet, their family-run farms are still the backbone of Guyana's agriculture.

Chinese and Europeans wield far greater influence than their small numbers might indicate. Like the East Indians, the Chinese and Portuguese came to Guyana as indentured workers. Those who stayed, however, opened small businesses or entered trades in cities and towns. For the most part, they adopted British ways and abandoned traditions from their homelands.

For years, the burden of indentured service kept both Chinese and Portuguese groups segregated from descendants of the first European colonists. Men often married African rather than European women. Their offspring contributed to a growing population of mixed ancestry. About 3 percent of the population claim mixed ancestry. Citizens of mixed races received various names. *Mulattoes* have at least one African ancestor. *Douglah* is the name given to children of African and East Indian parents.

Ten to 20 percent of Guyanese live out of the country. Many left to find better jobs and education. Although Guyanese have a high birthrate, the population decreased near the end of the twentieth century because of resettlement.

LANGUAGE

English is Guyana's official language, and it is spoken widely. A form of English, called Creole Patois, is also spoken. English serves to unify the country's diverse voices. Nevertheless, language distances Guyana from its neighbors. Guyana is the only South American country to conduct business and diplomatic relations in English.

Words from Amerindian, Creole, and East Indian languages slip into everyday speech. Words like *nyam* (eat), *repentir* (cemetery), and *foo-foo* (plantain) reflect Guyana's many origins. Some families speak only their original language in their homes. Different Amerindian tribes speak a form of Warrau, Arawak, or Carib. East Indians brought four languages with them as immigrants. A small percentage of East Indian families speak Hindi, Hindustani, Tamil, or Telagu.

RELIGION

Guyana's constitution guarantees religious freedom. Consequently, Christian churches, Muslim mosques, and Hindu temples coexist peacefully in the nation's cities and towns.

Fifty-one percent of the population, including most Guyanese of African, Chinese, and European descent, are Christian. Africans and Chinese follow Anglican practices introduced during colonial days by English landowners. Portuguese brought Roman Catholicism from their native land. The most widespread religion, Hindu, is observed by East Indians. A smaller percentage of East Indians are Muslim.

Major holidays of each religion are national events. These

An Islamic mosque (left) and a Hindu temple (right)

celebrations are the government's way of encouraging the Guyanese to accept and respect each other's differences.

Certain folk beliefs remain strong despite government laws against them. Obeah practices originated from African witchcraft and are common throughout the Caribbean. *Obeah* comes from an African word meaning "wizard." Obeah men or women claim unusual powers that allow them to speak with spirits who rid people of evil. Those who practice Obeah use bones, old rags, feathers, and blood to call upon the spirits and provide cures. Obeah leaders work their magic to restore health, promote love, and help believers with jobs and finances.

Some Amerindian tribes have their own medicine person, called *pai*. He protects individuals from evil spirits as do the wizards who practice Obeah. Many villagers wear lucky charms as added protection from evil spirits.

A number of little-known religious groups gained a following in Guyana. During the 1970s the government welcomed many from outside the country to show how different races can live together in peace. One cult from the United States was the People's Temple, led by Protestant clergyman Jim Jones. The People's Temple built a religious settlement called Jonestown in northwestern Guyana. In 1978, the United States government received reports of cult members being held against their will. Since a majority of the members were United States citizens, a California congressman, Leo Ryan, traveled to Jonestown to investigate. Jones felt threatened and ordered Ryan, three journalists, and an escaping cult member killed. Then Jones commanded his followers to drink poison. More than nine hundred cult members, including Jones, committed suicide in what became known as the Jonestown Massacre.

EDUCATION

Guyana inherited a strong school system from Great Britain. Since independence, however, the government has failed to build on those traditions. For decades, education followed political party lines. Teachers at the University of Guyana in Georgetown, the nation's main institution of higher learning, received promotions based on politics. Only professors with international standing advanced. The government mandated free education from nursery school to the university level. Yet schools lacked the funding to support the system. Many school buildings fell into sorry shape, and the number of qualified teachers, books, and supplies declined.

Today, children between ages four and fifteen must go to school. Students choose between academic, academic and technical, and vocational high schools. Even with these options,

*Two girls (left) from Sacred Heart Primary School
and teenage boys walking home from school (right)*

only about one-third of primary-grade students continue their
education. Still, more than 91 percent of Guyanese adults can read
and write, one of the highest rates in the region.

The government runs several trade schools that offer specialized
job training. The emphasis is on engineering, construction, and
other fields the country desperately needs. In 1985 the nation's
first boarding school, Presidents College, opened. The school
selects students who score in the top 2 percent on competitive
examinations. Guyana's schools must educate its future labor force
to survive in the twenty-first century.

HEALTH AND HOUSING

Government leaders continually support improving health
standards. As a result, Guyana's public health programs are
among the best in the nonindustrialized world. But heat, floods,

House in a rural village

and remote living conditions pose a severe threat during illness. Fifty-four out of every one thousand newborns die at birth. The average life span in Guyana is sixty-four years, compared with seventy-five years in the United States.

An organized network of hospitals, clinics, and visiting doctors and nurses supply medical care throughout the country. Rural maternal and child clinics offer preventive programs that focus on food quality, inoculation against disease, and self-help. Clinics reinforce the importance of proper sanitary conditions and safe drinking water to control disease.

Housing poses greater problems. Homes are poorly constructed of wood with iron or wooden shingles for roofs. Posts or concrete blocks lift the houses from the ground to avoid floods and mud. Some areas of Georgetown have electricity, but many low-income and most rural and plantation worker homes are without electricity and proper sanitation.

Guyanese eat many different rice dishes (left); cassava bread (right) is another staple.

FOODS

The Guyanese like to think of themselves as a "cook-up" society. The name derives from a dish called cook-up rice, a blend of different ingredients. Most typical Guyanese dishes, however, have a distinct flavor contributed by one of the country's many ethnic groups.

Amerindian pepper pot is a spicy stew of vegetables and meats. The stew is prepared in a pot that is always simmering. Cooks add new ingredients without ever emptying the pot. Oxtails and pigs' feet are two meats that might be added to the pot.

At festivals, English puddings, roast beef, and teas appear near Portuguese garlic pork and Chinese chow meins. Africans favor *metagee*, a mixture of yams and other underground root plants heated in coconut milk. And the smell of hot and spicy Indian curries is everywhere.

In rural areas, people eat more simply. Rice or potatoes with a meat or fish are eaten at the noontime main meal. Breads are made from starch of the cassava plant, and a drink is brewed from leaves of the soursop fruit.

Some of the crafts produced are hammocks, carved wooden art objects, and straw baskets.

THE ARTS

Guyanese express their origins through the arts. Amerindian crafts are usually functional. Men weave baskets and hammocks from jungle reeds. Amerindian women mold clay pots after pounding and moistening the dried earth. The complex designs decorating each object resemble patterns from long ago.

Modern Guyanese art usually delivers a message. Authors, painters, sculptors, and musicians communicate one of two themes through their art. Some artists glorify Guyana's wild beauty. Wilson Harris's first book, *Palace of the Peacock*, discusses the challenges of nature. Folk songs, such as "Itanamee," tell about gold prospecting and dazzling waterfalls.

The other theme depicts an aspect of the long struggle for

A painted clay vase

freedom and the value of ethnic identity. Two of Guyana's most notable painters are Denis Williams and Aubrey Williams. Both men settled in England but have painted powerful pictures about Guyana's stormy history. Sculptor Philip Moore is known for wooden forms based on African culture.

Many Guyanese novelists lived abroad but have written about their native country. Edgar Mittelholzer is the best known. His three novels called the *The Kwayana Family Trilogy* trace one Guyanese family through 350 years. E.R. Braithwaite told about his experiences as a black high school teacher in a tough London school. His story of troublesome race relations in *To Sir With Love* became a popular movie starring Sidney Poitier. Several Caribbean and English plays are performed yearly by the Guyana Theater Guild in Georgetown.

Calypso dancers at a festival

Each native group values its own music. Crude bamboo flutes and rawhide drums play songs for Amerindian ceremonies. Calypso music vibrates as dancers move rhythmically to steel drums. And East Indian classical kathak dancers stamp their bare feet to make the right sounds. India's most celebrated classical dancer is Guyanese-born Marlyn Hall Bose. Ms. Bose wears up to three hundred bells around her ankles and makes them sound in unison when she dances. Guyana's National Dance Company performs a variety of numbers with a multiethnic troupe.

SPORTS

Guyana's schools stress the importance of team sports. The most popular sport is cricket, a game something like baseball. The British introduced cricket to Guyana and its other colonies. Today,

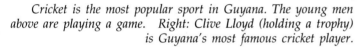
Cricket is the most popular sport in Guyana. The young men above are playing a game. Right: Clive Lloyd (holding a trophy) is Guyana's most famous cricket player.

local and professional clubs offer cricket as a favorite spectator sport. One of Guyana's most celebrated players was Clive Lloyd. Lloyd was the longest serving and most successful captain of the West Indies Cricket Team. He led the team to 36 victories and two Prudential World Cup finals.

Volleyball, tennis, and rugby, a form of football, draw large numbers of players. Each sport has local teams and clubs. There is a sports club for almost any sport. More than twenty sports associations oversee individual team events.

The Ministry of Education sponsors a National Sports Development Council to supervise formal sporting events. Each October the council holds Guyana's annual regatta, emphasizing the country's waterways. Athletes compete in swimming, water skiing, and boat races.

Above: Georgetown is at the mouth of the Demerara River. The alluvial soil that empties into the Atlantic gives the water a muddy look. Below: The harbor is busy with oceangoing traffic.

Georgetown

Chapter 8

A TRIP ALONG
THE WATERWAYS

GEORGETOWN

Guyanese call Georgetown their "Garden City," a town that grew along the eastern bank of the Demerara River. The city is Guyana's capital, major port, and manufacturing center. An estimated 180,000 people live within Georgetown's fifteen square miles (thirty-nine square kilometers), by far the largest city in the country. Georgetown is also the nation's first city, one that still reflects a strong colonial past.

Despite independence in 1966, Georgetown displays many signs of Dutch and English roots. Its name came from Britain's King George III. The Dutch contributed to Guyana's position as "the best laid out city in the Caribbean." Dutch settlers needed water to farm their long, rectangular sugar plantations. They dug canals for irrigation and surrounded them with streets that met at right

Above: Many houses in Georgetown are built along canals.
Below: Fishers gather up their nets at a seawall.

A typical brick dam

angles. Over the years, the original canals became wide, tree-lined avenues. The city assumed a checkerboard layout that remains today.

Georgetown sits below sea level. Massive walls built and improved by Dutch and English colonists extend the shoreline to hold back spring tides from the sea. Even with dams, floodgates, and wharf walls, flooding often limits travel along Guyana's coast.

Brickdam Street and a long park stretch along the sea walls. An important symbol of Guyana's freedom arches over this city's oldest avenue. The aluminum Independence Arch commemorates the date Guyana gained self-government from Britain.

Neighborhoods of houses on brick and wooden stilts merge into ornate public and religious buildings at the city's core. A business district runs parallel to the river. Guyana's buildings have always been constructed from wood. Major fires in 1945 and 1951 destroyed large sections of the wooden capital. Since then, plainer concrete buildings have replaced wood in burned-out areas.

Parliament building

Older sections of Georgetown exhibit an architectural wealth of buildings. Hand-carved details adorn wooden towers, balconies, windows, and porches with designs from the Victorian Age. The ornate Public Buildings house Parliament and offices for government officials. Inside is the old Council Chamber with rich dark woods and a carved ceiling. The chamber is where Prime Minister Forbes Burnham officially accepted the new constitution from Britain's Duke of Kent at independence.

In the heart of the city is St. George's Cathedral, the chief Anglican church in Guyana. The church is noted as the world's tallest wooden building. Its steeple rises 132 feet (40 meters) into the air. Nearby are the official President's Residence and Victoria Law Courts. Both display early classic style and cover spacious land.

A building typical of Amerindian construction is Umana Yana. The structure was built in 1972 to house the first conference of

The thatch building above is Umana Yana, *an Amerindian meeting place.*
St. George's Cathedral (inset)

nonaligned foreign ministers. *Umana Yana* means "meeting place of the people." The building serves as a gathering place, lounge, and recreation center. A team of Amerindians reproduced a cone-shaped, palm-thatch building similar to shelters found far within Guyana's interior. But Umana Yana occupies a larger area than most shelters—5,000 square feet (465 square meters).

Since independence, the government has revived Guyana's history through monuments. The Liberation Monument stands on the grounds of Umana Yana. Quartz pavement surrounds its five timber columns that stand behind a granite boulder. The memorial marks the struggle for freedom everywhere. These words are engraved on the boulder:

> "Mourn not for us who died
> But for our brothers everywhere
> Who live in bondage
> And mourning turn away to act."

Monument to the heroes of the 1763 Revolution (right); the Cenotaph (far right) dedicated to heroes of World Wars I and II

The 1763 Monument recalls the heroes of the 1763 Revolution against slavery and the plantation system. Philip Moore, African-Guyanese sculptor, carved the monument with features of West African religious art.

The Non-Aligned Monument stands in Company Path Garden. The government gave the land for the garden along with an adjoining old Anglican Cathedral to the city in 1907. The town council fenced the land with iron rails and planted a garden. The monument was erected in 1972 to honor the four founders of the nonaligned movement. President Arthur Chung, Guyana's president at the time, unveiled this tribute to President Nasser of Egypt; President Nkrumah of Ghana; Pandit Nehru, first president of India; and President Tito of Yugoslavia.

The Cenotaph is a marble shrine to those who died in World Wars I and II. The monument is 15 feet (4.6 meters) tall. On its

Just about anything can be found at Stabroek Market.

front is engraved the word "Sacrifice." Every year on Remembrance Day Guyanese leave wreaths to remember those who died in search of peace.

Goods are bought and sold in Georgetown's many markets. The most famous is Stabroek Market on Water Street. The oldest market, its name and style reflect Dutch influence. The market is built entirely of cast iron and extends over the Demerara River. Vendors bargain over prices from individual stalls in this bustling open supermarket. Visitors can buy anything here—from hand-crafted leather sandals and coconut shell jewelry to tropical fruits. Large amounts of gold are bought and sold at open markets. In Guyana someone must buy a gift of gold for every new baby. Even the poorest shoppers wear gold in earrings, chains, or barrettes.

Georgetown is Guyana's entertainment center. The National

The Botanic Garden and Zoo holds a band concert on Sunday afternoons (above). The garden is known for its collection of tropical flowers and palm trees (below).

Cultural Center has two theaters that seat two thousand viewers. Each theater exhibits murals and paintings by Guyanese artists. The center stages many local and international plays each year.

Strolling through gardens is a popular form of recreation in the city. The Botanic Gardens displays the greatest variety of tropical flowers and large collections of palms and lilies. John Frederick Woby first established the Botanic Gardens in 1878 with $72,000 voted by the government. For the next thirty-five years, Woby devoted himself to the garden. He amassed one of the most extensive tropical gardens in the Americas.

New and old Georgetown combine at the Timehri International Airport, located south of Georgetown on the right bank of the Demerara River. Local and international flights carry passengers to other countries and inland villages. One plan to attract more tourists is to expand and upgrade airport facilities.

The word *timehri* comes from an Amerindian word meaning "rock painting." The name refers to the rock engravings discovered near waterfalls and rapids in Guyana's interior. Amerindian legend claims that Timehri art came from the god Amalivaca. This deity visited Guyana at the time of a great flood. Historians believe the paintings were made by fourteenth-century Amerindians. Aubrey Williams, a celebrated Guyanese painter, decorated the outer wall of the airport's lounge with Timehri murals.

Georgetown comes alive during Mashramani with a grand series of events. For children there are mass games, a costume band display, and a people's parade. Calypso and steel bands compete, and East Indian dancers wearing bells ring in the holiday. Villagers travel to the city to hear the president's report and to experience the joys of Guyana.

City Hall in New Amsterdam

COASTAL TOWNS

The coastal road out of Georgetown passes through smaller villages before reaching a town of any size. New Amsterdam lies about 55 miles (89 kilometers) southeast of Georgetown. The town grew on the east bank of the Berbice River where it meets the Atlantic Ocean. New Amsterdam began as a settlement in 1792 when the Dutch left Fort Nassau farther up the Berbice. In 1891, New Amsterdam became an official town and the capital of Berbice County. Today, the city appears like a smaller Georgetown. Raised wooden houses stand on gridlike streets. Canals that remind visitors of its Dutch origins section the surrounding land.

New Amsterdam is Guyana's second-largest port city. More than twenty thousand people live in the town. Sugar, rice, cattle products, lumber, and bauxite from East and West Berbice territories travel from the city's docks. New Amsterdam is the core of Guyana's marketing operations.

Farther southeast in Guyana's East Berbice region is the town of Corriverton. This town is about 115 miles (185 kilometers) from Georgetown. The name is derived from the Courentyne River, where the town grew on the left bank.

Corriverton is a newer town of more than 30,000 people. The city has two major regions. Skeldon is a large sugar estate, and Springlands is a deepwater port. The town supports sugar, rice, lumber, and fishing industries.

Across the Essequibo River northwest of Georgetown is Anna Regina. The town was named after British Queen Anne, who reigned during the early eighteenth century. More recently, the city serves as administrative center for two western regions of Guyana. A large *koker*, or floodgate, protects the shores from seawater.

Ruins of Kijk-orver-al,
the first Dutch fort

LIVING INLAND

Few tourists venture to where the jungles of South America begin. Those who do, leave Georgetown by rickety minibus to the accompaniment of reggae music. The land out of town quickly transforms into rice paddies, sugarcane fields, and then rain forest. Once coastal roads end, voyagers depend on rivers and boat captains for travel.

Bartica is called the "Gateway to the Interior." This town of about ten thousand people is located where the Essequibo, Mazaruni, and Cuyuni rivers meet. Nearby are the ruins of Kijk-orver-al, the first Dutch fort, on an island in the Essequibo River.

A ship off-loading bauxite onto a larger ship in the Demarara River

The river's mouth is 20 miles (32 kilometers) wide and has
several islands about the size of Manhattan, a borough of New
York City. Many tales of fortune originate in Bartica. From here,
portnockers take steamers farther inland to prospect for gold and
diamonds in the Mazaruni Valley.

Inland about 67 miles (108 kilometers) up the Demerara River is
the town of Linden. This town resulted from merging the
communities of Mackenzie, Wismar, and Christianburg. Each
community was once a separate bauxite mining company. For
now, Linden maintains central bauxite mining operations for
Guymine, the national company. Most of the city's sixty thousand
people of working age earn their living mining and processing
bauxite. The Demerara River at Linden is deep enough to permit
oceangoing ships, and a paved road reaches inland from
Georgetown. Other inland developments, however, are cut off
from land travel and delivery of goods.

Mahdia is a settlement in the interior where many portnockers meet. The clear, smooth water leading to Mahdia is broken by rapids. Portnockers drag boats onto shore to walk around the dangerous fast current. Mahdia is typical of many inland villages. Buildings are raised wooden shacks of few rooms. The pace of living is generally relaxed. Goods cost five to six times more than in Georgetown. Truckers charge high prices to drive travelers and goods short distances because the roads are so pitted and muddy.

In the village of Abidine, a single tractor acts as delivery van, taxi, and hearse. Almost everything is airlifted into the region. For some settlements, the only link with the outside world is radio.

Schools, hospitals, and churches are missing from most villages. In their place are police stations and several bars. Portnockers work hard all day and like to party at night. In Abidine nighttime is for "sporting"–disco, pool, and backballing, a name for slow dancing to heavy drum beats. At the end of the day, everyone crawls into hammocks strung across a room to sleep.

Evidence of prospecting is everywhere. Portnockers post signs on trees to give notice of where and what they are mining. Dugout riverbeds and scratched rock formations prove the area has been mined. Even the beautiful Kaieteur Falls shows signs of wear. Ancient rock formations under its racing rapids promise a wealth of gold. But making a strike is less likely today.

THE FUTURE

The government sees great promise in the developing tourist trade. A seaplane flies visitors for about five hours from Georgetown to the falls. Plans are under way to expand lodging at and transportation to this and other beautiful sites.

A secondary waterfall in Kaieteur gorge

The natural beauty of the interior is Guyana's main attraction. Lush rain forests filled with valuable minerals and timber hold the nation's economic future. The greatest challenge, however, will be to unite a country born of many different cultures. Denis Williams, novelist and painter, believes Guyana has a bright outlook. In *Kyk-Over-Al Magazine* he wrote, "Guyanese . . . [are] capable of fashioning the universal. Beneath the sun which is all the color of the world walks the [person] who is all the races of the earth."

MAP KEY

Acarai Mountains	G13, G14
Anna Regina	D13
Atlantic Ocean	C12, C13, C14, D13, D14, E14
Barama (river)	D12, D13
Barima (river)	C13, D12, D13
Barima-Waini (province)	C12, C13, D12, D13
Bartica	D13
Berbice (river)	D14, E13, E14, F13
Burro Burro (river)	E13
Bush Lot	D14
Buxton	D13
Charity	D13
Corentyne (river)	E13, E14, F13, F14, G14
Corriverton	E14
Cuyuni (river)	D12, D13
Cuyuni-Mazaruni (province)	D12, D13, E12, E13
Dadanawa	F13
Demerara (river)	D13, E13
Demerara-Mahaica (province)	D13, D14
East Berbice-Corentyne (province)	D14, E13, E14, F13, F14, G13, G14
Enterprisé	D13
Essequibo (river)	D13, E13, F13, G13
Essequibo Islands-West Demerara (province)	D13
Fort Wellington	D14
Frederik Willem IV Vallen	F13, F14
Georgetown	D13
Holmia	E13
Hyde Park	D13
Ireng (river)	E12, E13
Isherton	F13
Issano	E13
Ituni	E13
Kaieteur Fall	E13
Kaieteur National Park	E13
Kaituma (river)	C13, D12, D13
Kako (river)	E12
Kamarang (river)	E12
Kamoa Mountains	G13
Kanuku Mountains	F13
Kassikaityu (river)	G13
Kuyuwini (river)	F13, G13
Kwitaro (river)	F13
Lethem	F13
Linden	D13, E13
Mabaruma	C13
Mahaica-Berbice (province)	D13, D14, E13, E14
Mahaicony Village	D14
Mahdia	E13
Makarapan Mountain (peak)	F13
Marina Fall	E13
Marlborough	D13
Matthews Ridge	D12
Mazaruni (river)	D12, D13, E13
Morawhanna	C13
New (river)	F14
New Amsterdam	D14
Oronoque (river)	F14, G14
Pakaraima Mountains	E12, E13
Paradise	D14
Parika	D13
Pomeroon (river)	D13
Pomeroon-Supenaam (province)	D13
Potaro (river)	E13
Potaro Landing	E13
Potaro-Siparuni (province)	E12, E13
Puruni (river)	D12, D13, E13
Queenstown	D13
Rewa (river)	E13, F13
Rockstone	E13
Rosehall	D14
Rosignol	D14
Rupununi (river)	F13
Saint Ignatius	F13
Spring Garden	D13
Suddie	D13
Takutu (river)	F13, G13
Tumatumari	E13
Upper Demerara-Berbice (province)	D13, E13, E14
Upper Takutu-Upper Essequibo (province)	E13, F13, G13
Vreed en Hoop	D13
Waini (river)	C13, D13
Wismar	E13

66° 10 64° 11 62° 12 60° 13 58° 14 56°

A

▽ 1742

L E S S E R   A N T I L L E S

CARRIACOU
GRENADINES
Victoria
Saint George's
GRENADA
▽ 570

ISLA LA ORCHILA (Ven.)
ISLA BLANQUILLA (Ven.)
ISLAS LOS HERMANOS (Ven.)
ISLAS LOS TESTIGOS (Ven.)

Speyside
TOBAGO
Scarborough
TRINIDAD
▽ 1379

B

NUEVA ESPARTA
ISLA DE MARGARITA
Juangriego
La Asunción
Porlamar
ISLA COCHE
PENÍNSULA DE PARIA
Río Caribe
Macuro
DRAGONS Mouths
PUNTA PIEDRAS
Port of Spain
Arima
Sangre Grande
TRINIDAD AND TOBAGO

A T L A N T I C

O C E A N

ISLA LA TORTUGA (Ven.)
Boca de Pozo
Punta de Piedras
ISLA CUBAGUA
CABO CODERA ▽ 1353
PUNTA DE ARAYA
Araya
Cumaná
Guanta
CUMANÁ
Casanay
Yoco
Güiria
Irapa
Yaguaraparo
El Pilar
Cariaco
Golfo de Cariaco
Carúpano
SUCRE
Gulf of Paria
San Fernando
Point Fortin
Princes Town
Siparia
GALEOTA POINT
Sangre Grande
GALERA POINT

la
DA
Río Chico
El Guapo
Puerto la Cruz
Barcelona
Pozuelos
Puerto Píritu
Clarines
Bergantín
San Mateo
Onoto
Aragua de Barcelona
Cumanacoa
Caripe
Aragua de Maturín
Caicara de Maturín
Quiriquire
Caripito
MONAGAS
MATURÍN
Jusepín
Cerro Turimiquire 2596
Punta de Mata
Amana
Guanipa
Tigre
Máximo
Caño Mánamo
DELTA DEL
Tucupita
ORINOCO
ISLA TOBÉJUBA
Boca Grande
COROCORO ISLAND
Morawhanna
Mabaruma
10°

ITAGRACIA
Orituco
San José de Guaribe
San Antonio de Tamanaco
Tamanaco
Valle de la Pascua
Espino
Santa María de Ipire
El Socorro
Zaraza
Valle de Guanape
Santa Ana
Cantaura
Pariaguán
ANZOÁTEGUI
San Tomé
San José de Guanipa
El Tigre
Mapire
Soledad
Ciudad Guayana
Orinoco
Caroní
Ciudad Bolívar
Largo
Temblador
Uracoa
Sacupana
Curiapo
Barrancas
DELTA AMACURO
Grande
Barima
Amacuro
Cuyubini
Waini
BARIMA-WAINI
Kaituma
Barima
Marlborough
Matthews Ridge
Barama
Pomeroon
Charity
Anna Regina
Queenstown
Suddie
Spring Garden
POMEROON SUPENAAM
ESSEQUIBO ISLANDS-WEST DEMERARA
Enterprise
Vreed en Hoop
GEORGETOWN
Parika
Buxton
Paradise
Hyde Park
Bartica
Mahaicony Village
Fort Wellington
Bush Lot
Rosignol
New Amsterdam
Rosehall
Corriverton
Nieuw Nickerie
Tofness
DEMERARA-MAHAICA
MAHAICA-BERBICE
8°

C

ICO
Valle de la Pascua
Moitaco
Upata
El Pao
El Palmar
Embalse de Guri
Guasipati
El Callao
El Manteco
El Perú
El Dorado
Tumeremo
Barama
Cuyuni
Cuyuni
CUYUNI-MAZARUNI
Mazaruni
Issano
Potaro Landing
Ituni
UPPER DEMERARA-BERBICE
Linden
Rockstone
Wismar
Berbice
Wageningen
NICKERIE
CORONIE
Apoera

D

Caicara de Orinoco
Maripa
Cerro Mato 1863
Las Bonitas
La Paragua
BOLÍVAR
Paragua
Canaima
Carrao
Caroní
Caroní
Cuyuni
Cuyuni
Kamarang
Kako
PAKARAIMA MOUNTAINS
MARINA FALL
KAIETEUR NATIONAL PARK
KAIETEUR FALL
Mahdia
Tumatumari
Holmia
POTARO-SIPARUNI
Orinduik
Corentyne
Corantijn
BLANCHE MARIE VALLEN
Bakhuis
NATUURRESERVAAT RALEIGHVALLEN VOLTZ BERG
SIPALIWINI
6°

E

AMAZONAS
Cerro Campanero △ 2200
Erebato
Cerro Guaiquinima 2100
SALTO ÁNGEL ANGEL FALLS
Auyán Tepuy 2950
Luepa
Irú Tepuy 2620
LA GRAN SABANA
Mount Roraima 2875
Cuquenán
Santa Elena de Uairén
PARQUE NACIONAL CANAIMA
Icabarú
Aponguao
Cotinga
Ireng
Maú
Burro Burro
WONOTOBO VALLEN
WILHELMINA GEB.
Juliana Top 1230
KAYSER GEBERGTE
SIPALIWINI

Cerro Yaví 2441
Cerro Uquía △ 2500
Cunucunuma
Cerro Marahuaca △ 2579
Cerro Duida △ 2400
La Esmeralda
Arabelo
Cacuri
Ventuari
Caura
Carutu
Paragua
Uraima
Metevari
Alcari
Uraricaá
ILHA DE MARACÁ
Uraricoera
Uraricoera
Conceição do Maú
Tacutu
Rupununi
Makarapan Mountain 934
Rewa
Essequibo
FREDERIK WILLEM IV VALLEN
East Berbice-Corentyne
Corentyne
Corantijn
Kabelebo
New
Nickerie
4°

F

SIERRA PARIMA
Matacuni
Padamo
Ocamo
Orinoco
Parima
Mucajaí
Apiaú
Mucajaí
Uraricoera
BRAZIL
BRASIL
GUYANA
Lethem
Saint Ignatius
KANUKU MOUNTAINS
Dadanawa
UPPER TAKUTU-UPPER ESSEQUIBO
Boa Vista
Branco
Kwitaro
Isherton
Kuyuwini
Essequibo
Lucie
Coeroeni
GUYANA
SURINAME
2°

G

VENEZUELA
Pico Tamacuari 2340
Siapa
Demini
Maquilaú
Negro
Cerro Avispa △ 2112
Pico da Neblina 3014
Araçá
Padauirí
Ajarani
Caracaraí
Bauaná
Anauá
Anauá
São José de Anauá
RORAIMA
Catrimani
Kassikaityu
KAMOA MOUNTAINS
ACARAI MOUNTAINS
Cafuini
Tauini
Kutari
Sipaliwini
Coeroeni
Poana
Corentyne
Aramu
Cemu
Marapi
Trombetas

MINI-FACTS AT A GLANCE

GENERAL INFORMATION

Official Name: Cooperative Republic of Guyana

Capital: Georgetown

Government: Guyana is a unitary multiparty republic with one legislative house, the National Assembly. The 53 members of the National Assembly are elected for 5 years and 12 members are appointed by the president to represent local and regional governments. The president is the head of state and head of the government. The prime minister also serves as the first vice-president of the Assembly. The highest judicial body is the Court of Appeal. For administrative purposes the country is divided into ten regions.

Religion: Guyana does not officially support any religion; the constitution guarantees religious freedom to all. About 38 percent of the people are Hindus, followed by 35 percent Protestants, 15 percent Roman Catholics, 5 percent Muslims, and 7 percent who claim no religious affiliation. Some folk beliefs originating from African witchcraft are practiced despite government laws against them.

Ethnic Composition: Guyana's population includes six main ethnic groups–Amerindians (indigenous Indians of the Americas), East Indians (descendants of settlers from the Indian subcontinent), Africans, Chinese, Europeans who are mostly Portuguese and English, and people with mixed racial background. The largest ethnic group is East Indians with 52 percent of the population; followed by black Africans, 40 percent; Amerindians (Arawaks, Makus, Warraus, Caribs), 5 percent; and mixed race, mulattoes and douglahs, 3 percent.

Language: English is the official language and is spoken widely; it is the language of commerce, government, schools, and the press. Hindustani, Creole Patois, Chinese, Portuguese, Tamil, Telagu, and some Amerindian languages (Warrau, Arawak, and Carib) are spoken also.

National Flag: The national flag is known as "the Golden Arrowhead." A red triangle at the hoist extends to the flag's midpoint and is bordered on the two sides by a narrow black stripe. Extending from this red triangle is a golden arrowhead pointing toward the fly; it is bordered by a narrow white stripe on two sides. Two green triangles make up the rest of the flag. The green stands for Guyana's forests, golden yellow for its mineral resources, white for the country's many rivers, red for the energy of the people, and black for their perseverance.

National Emblem: A white shield is flanked by two jaguars, one holding a sugarcane stalk and the other a miner's pickax. The shield is divided by three wavy blue lines. The hoatzin bird (Guyana's national bird) decorates the bottom part and the Victoria Regia lily decorates the top part of the shield. Beneath the emblem is the national motto "One People, One Nation, One Destiny" on a red and gold ribbon.

National Anthem: Begins "Great land of Guyana"

National Calendar: Gregorian

Money: Guyana dollar (G$) of 100 cents is the basic unit. In March 1994 one G$ was worth $0.0076 in United States currency.

Membership in International Organizations: Caribbean Common Market (CARICOM); Caribbean Sugar Products and Exporters Association; Economic Commission For Latin America and the Caribbean (ECLAC); Inter-American Development Bank (IDB); International Bauxite Organization; International Sugar Association; Organization of American States (OAS); United Nations (UN)

Weights and Measures: Guyana officially adopted the metric system in 1982 but imperial measures are still in general use.

Population: 1993 estimates total 815,000; density 10 persons per sq. mi. (4 persons per sq km); 65 percent rural, 35 percent urban.

Cities:

Georgetown	150,000
Linden	35,000
New Amsterdam	25,000
Corriverton	13,800
Bartica	6,200

(Population figures based on 1985 estimates, except for Corriverton and Bartica, which are based on 1980 estimates.)

GEOGRAPHY

Border: Guyana is bounded by the Atlantic Ocean to the north, Suriname to the east, Brazil to the south and southwest, and Venezuela to the northwest.

Coastline: 270 mi. (435 km)

Land: The country is located just north of the equator on the northeastern coast of South America. Guyana has four distinct physical regions: coastal plain, hilly sand and clay belt, interior savannas, and highlands. Much of the 2 to 30 mi. (3 to 48 km) wide coastal plain in the north is below high-tide level; a 140 mi. (225 km) long seawall holds water back from crops and homes. The hilly sand and clay belt is covered with dense tropical forests. These sandy hills form the largest region in Guyana, covering about 85 percent of the country. Two separate flat and dry grassy plains (savannas) cover about 10 percent of Guyana. The Guyana highlands are part of the oldest geological formations in South America. The Pakaraima Mountain range is in the western frontier.

More than 90 percent of the population lives on 5 percent of the land along the Atlantic coast. The densely forested interior is almost uninhabited.

Highest Point: Mount Roraima at 9,094 ft. (2,772 m)

Lowest Point: 5 ft. (1.5 m) below sea level along the Atlantic coast

Rivers: There are several large rivers, including the Essequibo, Demerara, Courantyne, and Berbice, all flowing from south to north. Only a few are navigable for any distance because of rapids and falls. The Courantyne River makes Guyana's eastern border with Suriname. The coast is cut by several short rivers such as Pomeroon, Mahaica, Mahaicony, and Abary.

Guyana has some of the most spectacular waterfalls in the world including the Kaieteur Fall on the Potaro River, the highest single-drop waterfall in the world; King George VI Falls on the Utashi River; and the Great Falls on the Mazaruni River.

Forests: Some 85 percent of the land is forested. The coastal area has long been cleared of swamp and marshes for farming. The forests contain about 1,000 different varieties of trees including the greenheart tree, the most valuable timber for construction. The greenheart and wallaba hardwood timber resist termites, decay, and moisture and are practically indestructible. Siruaballi, hubaballi, and balata hardwoods are used for furniture. Giant mora and crabwood trees grow on swampy sites. The savanna grows clusters of grass and scattered palm trees. Orchids, Spanish moss, and pineapple epiphyte plants are widespread. The Victoria Regia lily leaves grow up to 6 ft. (1.8 m) wide in still ponds; it is Guyana's national flower. The Kaieteur National Park is the only major conservation area.

Wildlife: A variety of tropical wildlife is found in Guyana. The most common animals are monkeys, deer, anteaters, armadillos, tapir, jaguars, caymans, turtles, and peccaries (pigs). Locusts, acoushi ants, and bats are prevalent. There are almost 780 species of birds including the hummingbird, vulture, kingfisher, greenheart, tinamou, and bellbird. The hoatzin is a rare bird found chiefly in Guyana. Sea turtles breed on the northwestern coastal beaches. The manatee enjoys protective status as an endangered species.

Climate: Guyana's tropical climate is marked by hot and rainy weather and high humidity all year round. Inland temperatures range from 66° to 103° F. (18.8° to 39.4° C), and coastal temperatures vary from 74° to 86° F. (23.3° to 30° C). Rainfall is heaviest along the coast and in the highlands. Annual rainfall averages 91 in. (230 cm) along the coast to 60 in. (150 cm) in the southwest. There are two rainy seasons in the north, May to July and November to January, and one in the southwest, from April to August. Heavy rainfall sometimes causes extreme flooding. The country experiences very few other natural disasters like tornadoes, hurricanes, or earthquakes.

Greatest Distance: North to South: 495 mi. (797 km)
East to West: 290 mi. (467 km)

Area: 83,000 sq. mi. (214,969 km)

ECONOMY AND INDUSTRY

Agriculture: Agriculture is the chief economic activity for about one-third of the population. Most farmers work with hand tools and use water buffalo or oxen to haul plows or wagons; tractors are used to move sugarcane to processing plants. Land reclaimed from the sea is fertile but acidic; lost fertility must be returned to the soil by periodic fallowing or the addition of fertilizers. Farmers largely depend on rainfall and floods for irrigation. Guyana's most important crop is sugarcane; it is grown on large plantations. The second most-important crop is rice; other crops are citrus fruits, cocoa, cassava, corn, coconuts, coffee, and plantains (similar to bananas).

Farmers raise beef and dairy cattle, goats, sheep, pigs, and chickens in the

Rupununi Savanna. Some ham and bacon are processed. Coastal shrimp and fish from inland streams form the basis of a limited but growing fishing industry. Common fish are lukanani, haimara, pacu, biara, snapper, eel, and grouper. The giant freshwater piraucu fish attains lengths up to 14 ft. (4.3 m).

Mining: Bauxite is Guyana's most valuable mineral and the leading export. It is mined from under the white sand and clay shores of the Demerara River and is refined into aluminum. Bauxite exports account for some one-third of the country's total exports. Manganese is dug from the plateau at Arakaka on the Barima River. Other minerals found in smaller quantities are diamonds, gold, copper, iron ore, molybdenite, nickel, white sand (used in glass manufacturing), kaolin (China clay), and graphite. A large gold mine was located in the Essequibo region in the early 1990s; when in full operation this will be one of the largest gold mines in South America. Oil is being explored in the Rupununi Savanna. Electricity is largely generated from imported oil.

Manufacturing: Manufacturing in Guyana is limited. The main activities are bauxite, rice, livestock feed, tobacco, and timber processing, and manufacturing of bricks, tires, soaps, and clothing. Sugarcane by-products are used in the processing of rum, molasses, syrups, medical and industrial alcohols, paper products, and fuel. Alcoholic beverages and pharmaceuticals are becoming important.

Transportation: Guyana has a total length of 60 mi. (97 km) of privately owned railroads used for mineral transportation. In the early 1990s Guyana had a total road length of 3,540 mi. (5,697 km) of which 11 percent was paved. Most of the roads are in the coastal regions; roads are poor or nonexistent through dense forests. A few unpaved trails extend into the savanna. The Harbor Bridge over the Demerara River is one of the longest (6,074 ft.; 1,851 m) floating bridges in the world. Guyana Airways Corporation is the national airline and the only international airport is at Timehri near Georgetown, which is also served by KLM, the Dutch international airline. Chief seaports are at Georgetown, New Amsterdam, and Springlands. Ferry and steamer services offer transportation along the coast. Barges and small boats carry people and agricultural products in the canals of the coastal estates and villages. Minibuses, taxis, and cycles provide transportation in urban areas.

Communication: Though still under government control, Guyana's television, radio, and newspapers have experienced greater freedom of expression since 1985. *The Guyana Chronicle* is the only daily newspaper. Telegraph service connects Guyana with the United States. In the early 1990s there was one radio receiver per 2.4 persons, one television set per 19 persons, and one telephone per 47 persons.

Trade: Chief imports are petroleum, machinery, vehicles, cloth, footwear, food, and other consumer goods. Major import sources are the United States, the United Kingdom, Trinidad and Tobago, Japan, and Canada. Chief export items are sugar, bauxite, aluminum, diamonds, gold, rice, shrimp, molasses, rum, and timber. Major export destinations are the United States, the United Kingdom, Canada, Japan, and the Netherlands.

EVERYDAY LIFE

Health: Guyana's public health program includes an organized network of hospitals, clinics, and visiting doctors and nurses supplying medical care throughout the country. Malaria has been virtually eliminated as a major health problem, but yellow fever is still a threat. In 1990 there were one physician per 6,800 persons and one hospital bed per 350 persons. Some Amerindians have their own medicine person, called *pai*, who protects individuals from evil spirits. Life expectancy is 61 years for males and 68 years for females. Infant mortality rate at 54 per 1,000 births is high.

Education: Education is officially compulsory and is provided free of charge for children between ages 4 and 15. After nursery school, primary education begins and lasts for six years. Students choose between academic, technical, and vocational high schools. There are some 15 technical, teacher training, vocational, special, or higher education institutions. The University of Guyana has faculties in agriculture, the arts, health sciences, social sciences, education, and technology. Presidents College, the country's only boarding school, draws its students by nationwide competitive examination from the top 2 percent of Guyana's schoolchildren. In the early 1990s the literacy rate was reported to be more than 90 percent.

Holidays:
New Year's Day, January 1
Republic (Mashramani) Day, February 23
Labor Day, May 1
Caribbean Day, 1st Monday in July
Freedom Day, 1st Monday in August
United Nations Day, October 24
Christmas Day, December 25
Boxing Day, December 26

Moving religious holidays include Good Friday, Easter Monday, Holi Phagwah, Deepawali, Id al-Adha, and Yaoumun Nabi.

Culture: The National Library in Georgetown is also a public library with about 35 branches. The Guyana Society Library is the oldest in the country and has a collection of rare books dealing with Amerindians. The Guyana Museum in Georgetown has a collection of flora and fauna and national archaeological findings. Several ornate public buildings house government offices in Georgetown. St. George's Cathedral in Georgetown is noted as the world's tallest wooden building.

Traditional handicrafts involve wood, leather, and clay. Amerindian men weave baskets and hammocks from jungle reeds; the women mold clay pots decorated with complex designs.

Society: Guyanese society is predominantly rural; it is also a reflection of its diverse ethnic makeup. Traditionally Amerindians have not been part of Guyana's social, political, or economic scene, as they were living a secluded life in the forests. More recently, larger numbers of Amerindians have migrated to cities and towns and have jobs on cattle farms, in mines, or teaching and nursing. Most of the Africans are descendants of slaves captured from the coast of West Africa. Women from African-Guyanese society are very independent. East Indian population has strong family ties and cultural bonds with India. Their family-run farms are still the backbone of Guyana's agriculture. The East Indians have done well in trade and are well represented among the professions. Chinese and Portuguese who also came to Guyana as indentured workers, have for the most part adopted British ways and left traditions from their homelands behind.

Dress: Most of the Guyanese wear informal Western-style clothing. Some East Indian women wear a *sari*, several yards of lightweight cloth draped around the body. Amerindian men and women wear sandals and simple body cover-ups. They decorate their bodies with arm and leg bands, jewelry, and paints made from vegetable dyes and animal oils. Amerindians who have moved to cities and towns wear Western clothes.

Housing: A shortage of housing is a critical problem in urban areas. A number of government housing programs, like low-cost rental housing, are operating in Georgetown and New Amsterdam. Homes are constructed of wood with iron or wooden shingles for roofs. Flammable wood structures in Georgetown have been consumed in disastrous fires and now are being replaced with other materials. Some areas of Georgetown have electricity, but the poorer neighborhoods lack electricity and running water. Many low-income and most rural and plantation worker homes are without electricity and other modern conveniences. Lack of adequate water supplies and effective waste disposal is a problem in the major urban areas.

In villages wood and concrete-block dwellings are usually built on stilts above the flood-prone land and are connected with footbridges to the streets; these streets are built over the drainage and irrigation canals. Some Amerindians build thatch homes on stilts to avoid flood and insects while some live in villages of round homes.

Food: Most Guyanese dishes have a distinct flavor of one of the country's ethnic groups. A spicy soup of vegetables and meats called pepper pot is an Amerindian dish; the pot is always simmering and is never emptied. English puddings, roast beef, garlic pork, *metagee* (a mixture of yams and other underground root plants cooked in coconut milk), and spicy Indian curries are the most common dishes. People drink tea at all occasions.

Sports and Recreation: Cricket is the national and most favorite spectator sport. Other games include volleyball, tennis, and rugby (a form of football). Guyana's annual regatta emphasizes the country's waterways; athletes compete in swimming, water skiing, and boat races. Much recreational activity is based upon the festivities accompanying Hindu, Muslim, and Christian holidays. Strolling through gardens is a popular form of recreation in Georgetown. Steel drums and bands play Calypso music at festivals. East Indian classical dance and music also are popular. Bamboo flutes and rawhide drums are used in Amerindian music. Guyana's National Dance Company, with a multiethnic troupe, performs a variety of numbers.

Social Welfare: A national insurance scheme, compulsory for most workers and employers, has been in place since 1969. Some self-employed people also are covered under this scheme. In the East Indian community family members generally take care of their elderly and poor relatives. Rural maternal and children's clinics offer preventive programs that focus on the quality of food, inoculations, and self-help.

IMPORTANT DATES

1498–Christopher Columbus sights the land of present-day Guyana and calls it "Guiana"

1499–Alonso de Ojeda, one of Christopher Columbus' mapmakers, returns to Guiana's coast

1530–Pedro de Acosta brings a Spanish expedition

1581–The Dutch establish a settlement and claim Guiana

1596–Sir Walter Raleigh, an English explorer, writes *The Discoverie of the large and bewtiful Empire of Guiana*

1616–Dutch and English settlers build the first permanent settlement called Kijk-orver-al

1621–Dutch West India Company is in control of the colony

1738–Dutch West India Company appoints Laurens Storm van Gravesande as secretary

1763–Cuffy, a house slave, organizes a revolt against plantation owners

1770–Some 15,000 Africans are in slavery in the Demerara sugar region under Dutch control

1781–Britain seizes Berbice, Essequibo, and Demerara from the Dutch

1792–Settlement of New Amsterdam begins

1807–The British Parliament orders an end to the slave trade

1814–Britain gains control of Guiana

1823–More than 200 slaves die in the East Coast Insurrection

1834–Britain forms the colony of British Guiana; slavery is abolished in British colonies

1835–Britain sends German explorer and botanist Robert Schomburgk to mark the colony's boundaries

1837–Schomburgk discovers the Victoria Regia water lily

1838–The first 396 East Indian immigrants arrive in Guiana

1848–Coastal railways are established in Guiana, the first railway lines in South America

1849–Only 180 of 230 sugar plantations and 16 of 174 coffee and tobacco farms are in operation

1876–Compulsory Education Act is passed

1878–John F. Woby establishes the Botanic Gardens in Georgetown

1880–Gold is discovered in the disputed area claimed by both Guiana and Venezuela

1891–Britain lowers income qualifications for service and expands the colonial governor's power; New Amsterdam becomes an official town and capital of Berbice County

1899–Disputed area with Venezuela is awarded to Guiana

1905–British Guiana starts exporting rice

1907–The government gives land to the city of Georgetown for a garden

1917–The practice of bringing indentured workers from India, China, and Portugal is stopped; the first bauxite mine opens

1922–The British Guiana labor union protests overtime work without overtime pay

1928–The British Parliament orders its colonies to recognize labor unions

1935–British Guiana holds elections

1938-39–Lord Moyne investigates the social and economic problems of British Guiana and writes an 800-page report

1943–The constitution is revised

1945–Fire destroys large sections of Georgetown

1947–British Guiana holds elections

1948–Sugar workers lead a peaceful strike for better wages and work conditions

1950–The number of eligible male voters climbs to 4,312 from a meager 916 in 1850

1951–Fire once again destroys sections of Georgetown

1953–National elections are held, the People's Progressive Party (PPC) wins 18 out of 24 seats; Britain suspends the constitution and removes President Cheddi B. Jagan and his administration from office

1955–Linden Forbes Sampson Burnham officially breaks from the PPC and forms a new party called the People's National Congress (PNC)

1957–National elections are held; Jagan is elected president

1961–Jagan is reelected president

1962–Violence breaks out between East Indians and Africans

1963–The University of Guyana is opened; Great Britain calls a constitutional convention

1964–National elections are held; a coalition government is formed

1966–Guyana becomes a self-governing dominion within the Commonwealth; Guyana joins the United Nations; Venezuela claims land west of the Essequibo River

1967–The University of Guyana awards its first degrees; international telex service is inaugurated

1968–Timehri International Airport is established

1969–National Social Insurance Scheme is introduced; Rupununi Rebellion is suppressed; there are border clashes with Suriname

1970–Guyana becomes a cooperative republic; the post of governor-general is abolished; Kuru Kuru Cooperative College is established

1971–Demerara Bauxite Company is nationalized

1972–The Umana Yana building in the Amerindian style is constructed in Georgetown to house the first conference of nonaligned foreign ministers

1973–Guyana Cooperative Mortgage Finance bank is established; legislation is passed restricting freedom of movement; the Caribbean Common Market (CARICOM) replaces the Caribbean Free Trade Association (CARIFTA)

1974–Guyana Housing Corporation is established; the Declaration of Sophia transforms PNC into a socialist party

1975–Reynolds Guyana Mines are nationalized

1976–The government assumes responsibility for all church and private schools; Booker Sugar Estates are nationalized

1977–A strike by sugar workers becomes violent as the government uses police to stop the strike

1978–Guyana signs the eight-nation Amazon Pact; the Jonestown Massacre takes place, United States Representative Leo J. Ryan and two journalists are killed by cult members of the People's Temple; later more than 900 cult members commit suicide

1980–A new constitution is adopted; Guyana adopts a presidential form of government; Burnham becomes president

1982–Guyana adopts the metric system

1983–Guyana and Venezuela refer the land dispute to the United Nations; Guyana condemns United States invasion of Grenada

1985–Presidents College, the country's first boarding school, is opened; President Burnham dies; national elections are held and Hugh Desmond Hoyte becomes president

1986–Guyana receives non-voting status in the Organization of American States (OAS)

1987–Vice-president General Mohamed Shahabuddeen is elected to the International Court of Justice

1988–The International Monetary Fund (IMF) begins negotiations for economic assistance to Guyana

1990–Guyana starts receiving IMF assistance

1991–Guyana becomes a member of OAS

1992–Guyana restores diplomatic relations with Israel and establishes relations with El Salvador; general elections are held; Jagan wins presidency; Guyana signs a tax information exchange agreement with the United States; the Guyana $500 note is put into circulation for the first time

IMPORTANT PEOPLE

Accabre, slave who helped to organize the Berbice Slave Rebellion in 1763 with Cuffy and Akara

Akara, slave who helped to organize the Berbice Slave Rebellion in 1763

Marlyn Hall Bose, Indian classical dancer

Edward Ricardo Braithwaite (1912-1985), novelist; major works include *To Sir With Love*

Linden Forbes Sampson Burnham (1923-85), an African-Guyanese lawyer; former leader of the People's National Congress (PNC); one of the leading figures in Guyana politics from 1964 until his death in 1985

Jan Carew (1925-   ), poet and novelist; major work is *Black Midas*

Martin Carter (1927-   ), poet

Hubert N. Critchlow, considered father of local trade unionism; led the development of organized labor

Cuffy, house slave who organized the Berbice Slave Rebellion at the Magdalenenburg Plantation

Peter d'Aguiar (1912-   ), political leader of the Portuguese party

Ayube Edun, British-educated East Indian; organized the Man-Power Citizens Association (MPCA), a successful sugar worker's union

Hamilton Green (1904-   ), prime minister in 1985

Wilson Harris (1921-   ), writer; works include *Palace of the Peacock*

Sam Hinds (1933-   ), prime minister in 1993

Hugh Desmond Hoyte (1930-   ), president in 1985

Cheddi Berret Jagan, Jr. (1918-   ), dentist, founder of the People's Progressive Party (PPP); chief minister from 1957 to 1961; prime minister from 1961 to 1964; elected president in 1992

Janet Rosenberg Jagan, American-born wife of Cheddi B. Jagan; moved to British Guiana in 1943; active in the formation of PPP; the first woman elected to the Guyana legislature

Clive Lloyd, Guyana's most celebrated cricket player; one of the most successful captains of the West Indies Cricket Team; led the team to 36 victories and two Prudential World Cup finals

Edgar Mittelholzer (1909-65), novelist; major works include the "Kwayana Trilogy"

Philip A. Moore (1918-   ), sculptor; his wooden sculptures show African influence; works include the monument dedicated to the Berbice Slave Rebellion in downtown Georgetown

Christopher Nicole, novelist; works include *Ratoon*

A.G. Seymour (1927-   ), poet and writer; works include *I was Born in Georgetown*

General Mohamed Shahabuddeen (1939-   ), political figure; elected to the International Court of Justice in 1987

John Frederick Woby, established the Botanic Garden that is now one of the most extensive tropical gardens in the Americas

Aubrey Williams (1922-1990), painter; decorated the outer wall of the Timehri international airport lounge with murals

Denis Williams (1941-   ), painter, novelist, curator, and anthropologist

Clinton Wong, Chinese-born businessman; senior vice-chairman of PPP

Compiled by Chandrika Kaul

A home built on stilts in the Essequibo River

INDEX

Page numbers that appear in boldface type indicate illustrations

Abary River, 110
Abidine, 104
Accabre, 35, 120
administrative regions, 59, 108
Africans, 8, 34, **74,** 77-79, **77,**
    108, 114
agriculture, **6,** 7, 14, 15, 21, 28-29,
    28, 33, 35, 36, 37, **38,** 42, **43,**
    44, 61-65, **62, 63, 64,** 111-112
air travel, 72-73, **72,** 99, 112
Akara, 35, 120
aluminum, 70, 112
Amazon Pact, 119
Amerindians, 7, 8, 17, **17,** 27-29,
    28, 29, 32, 49, 56, **74,** 75-77, 80,
    86, 108, 114, 115
animals, 24-25, **24, 25,** 111
Anna Regina, 101
Anne, Queen, 101
anteaters, 24, **24,** 111
anthem, national, 9, 109
apprenticeship system, 40
Arakaka, 16
arapaimas, 24
Arawak Indians, 27, 28-29, 76,
    76, 80, 108
armadillos, 24, 111
arts, 86-88, **86, 87, 88,** 114
Atlantic coast, 110
Atlantic Ocean, 13, 15, 101
balata, 23, 110
Barima River, 16, 30
Bartica, 102-103, 109
bauxite, 16, 44, 61, 65, **65,** 70,
    103, 112, 117
bellbird, **24,** 25
Berbice Colony, 35, 36, 37, 116
Berbice County, 101, 117
Berbice River, 15, 16, 32, 65, 72,
    101, 110
Berbice Slave Rebellion, 34-35,
    53, 116
birds, 24, **24,** 25, **25,** 111
Booker Group of Companies, 70
Booker Sugar Estates, 119
borders, 13, 110

border conflict, 13, 56-57
Bose, Marlyn Hall, 88, 120
Botanic Gardens, **98,** 99, 117
Braithwaite, Edward Ricardo, 87,
    120
Brazil, 13, 15, 17, 19, 57
British Guiana, 37, 39-49, 117,
    118
British Guiana Laborer Union,
    45
Burnham, Linden Forbes
    Sampson, 47-49, 51, 52-53, **52,**
    57, 94, 118, 119, 120
calendar, 109
Calypso music, 88, **88**
Capital. *See* Georgetown
Carew, Jan, 120
Carib Indians, 27, 28, 76, 80
Caribbean Common Market
    (CARICOM), 58, 70, 109, 119
Caribbean Free Trade
    Association (CARIFTA), 58, 119
Caribbean Islands, 30
Caribbean Sugar Products and
    Exporters Association, 109
Carter, Jimmy, 55
Carter, Martin, 120
caymans, 24, 111
celebrations, **4,** 8-9, **9,** 11, 80-81,
    85, 99, 113-114, 115
Cenotaph, 96-97, **96**
Charity, 71
Chinese, 8, 41-42, 79, 108
Christians, 80
Christianburg, 103
Chung, Arthur, 96
Cleveland, Grover, 56-57
climate, 20-21, 111
coastal plain, 14-15, 64, 110
coastline, 13, 110
coat of arms, 10, **10, 52**
Columbus, Christopher, 29-30,
    30, 115
Combined Court, 37, 43-45
communication, 73, 112
Company Path Garden, 96

Compulsory Education Act of
  1876, 42, 117
constitution, 46, 52, 53, 59, 80,
  108, 117, 119
Corriverton, 101, 109
Council Chamber, 94
Courantyne River, 15, 16, 71,
  101, 110
Court of Appeal, 59, 108
Court of Policy, 37
Creole Patois, 80
Critchlow, Hubert, 44-45, 120
Cuffy, 35, 53, 116, 120
culture, 114
Cuyuni, 32, 102-103
d'Aguiar, Peter, 51, 120
de Acosta, Pedro, 30, 116
Declaration of Sophia, 119
Deepavali, 11
deer, 24, 111
Demba, 65
Demerara, 36, 37, 116
Demerara Bauxite Company, 119
Demerara River, 15, 16, 32, 36,
  41, 44, 65, 69, 71, **90,** 91, 97,
  99, 103, **103,** 110, 112
de Ojeda, Alonso, 115
diamonds, 44, 78, 112
dikes, 33
*Discoverie of the large and bewtiful
  Empire of Guiana* (Raleigh), 31,
  116
douglahs, 79, 108
dress, 114
D'Urban, Benjamin, 37
Dutch, 7, 14, 30, 32-34, **32,** 36,
  37, 91, 101, 116
Dutch West India Company, 32,
  32, 116
East Coast Insurrection, 40, 116
East Indians, 8, 42-43, 49, **74,**
  78-79, 80, 108, 114, 116
Economic Commission for Latin
  America and the Caribbean
  (ECLAC), 109
Economic Recovery Plan, 54
economy, 8, 16, 44, 45, 53, 54-55,
  61

education, 8, **9,** 42-43, 82-83, **83,**
  88, 113
Edun, Ayube, 45, 121
El Dorado, 31-32
elections, 46, 49, 52-53, 55, 117,
  118
electric eels, 24
elevation, 19, 110
El Salvador, 120
emblem, national, 7, 10, 109
emigration, 54
English language, 80, 108
Enmore, 47
epiphytes, 23, **23**
Essequibo, 36, 37, 67, 112, 116
Essequibo River, 15, **15,** 16, 32,
  56, 71, 72, 101, 102-103, 110,
  118, **122**
ethnic groups, 7-8, **74,** 75-79, **76,**
  77, 78, 108
European exploration, 29-32
everyday life, 113-115
falls, **12, 18,** 19, 69, 104, 110
fire, 93, 118
fishing, 24-25, 68-69, **69, 93,** 112
flag, 10-11, 108-109
flooding, 14, **14,** 33
foods, **60,** 64, 85, **85,** 115
foreign relations, 57-58, 120
forests, 16, 67-68, **68,** 110
Fort Nassau, 101
French, 36
French Guiana, 13, 36
future, 104-105
geography, 7, 13-17, **18,** 19-20,
  19, 20, 110-111
George III, King, 37, 91
Georgetown, 8, 35, 37, **37,** 41, 47,
  49, 53, **59, 60,** 68, **69,** 70, 71,
  72, 73, **78,** 82, 84, 87, **90,** 91,
  92, 93-97, **93, 94, 95, 96, 97, 98,**
  99, 103, 104, 109, 112, 114, 117
gold, 42, 44, 56, 66-67, **66,** 78,
  112, 117
government, 58-59, 108
Gravesande, Laurens Storm van,
  35-36, 116
Great Britain, 7, 8, 35-37, 49, 56, 116

Great Depression, 45
Great Falls, 19, 110
Green, Hamilton, 121
greenheart tree, 16, 21, 25, 68, **68,** 110
Grenada, 119
Guyana Airways Corporation, 72-73, 112
Guyana Cooperative Mortgage Finance bank, 119
Guyana Fisheries Company, 68
Guyana Housing Corporation, 119
Guyana Mining Enterprise, 65
Guyana Museum, 114
Guyana Society Library, 114
Guyana Theater Guild, 87
Guymine, 65, 103
Guysuco, 63
Harbor Bridge, 71, 112
Harris, Wilson, 86, 121
health, 83-84, 113
High Court Building, **59**
highlands, 16-17, 19, 110
hills, 16, 110
Hinds, Sam, 121
Hindus, 11
history, 7-9, 27-59, 115-120
hoatzin, 10, **25,** 111
holidays, **9,** 11, 80-81, 113-114, 115
housing, **5,** 27-28, 84, **84,** 114-115, 122
Hoyte, Hugh Desmond, 53-54, **54,** 119, 121
hubaballi, 23, 110
hummingbirds, 25, 111
hydroelectric power, 16, 65, 69
indenture system, 40-42, 43, 44, 79, 117
independence, 8, **9, 50,** 51-52, 57
Independence Arch, 93
India, 57
industry, 68-70, 112
Inter-American Development Bank (IDB), 109
International Bauxite Organization, 70, 109

International Court of Justice, 58, 120
International Monetary Fund (IMF), 120
international organization, 54, 109
International Sugar Association, 109
Israel, 120
Ituni, 65
Jagan, Cheddi Berret, 46-48, **48,** 49, 51, 52, 55-56, **55,** 73, 118, 120, 121
Jagan, Janet Rosenberg, 46-48, **48,** 121
jaguars, 111
James, King, 32
Jones, Jim, 82
Jonestown Massacre, 82, 119
Kaieteur Falls, **18,** 19, 72, 104, 110
Kaieteur National Park, 111
Kanuku Mountains, 17, 20
Kijk-orver-al, 32, 102, **102,** 116
kingfisher, 25
King George VI Falls, 19, 110
Kuru Kuru Cooperative College, 118
Kwakwani, 65
Kwayana Family Trilogy (Mittelhozer), 87
language, 80, 108
Latin American and Caribbean Sugar Producers and Exporters Association, 70
Liberation Monument, 95
Libya, 57
Linden, **65,** 103, 109
livestock, 64-65, 111-112
Lloyd, Clive, 89, **89,** 121
Longchamps, 36
Mackenzie, 65, 103
Magdalenenburg Plantation, 35
Mahaica River, 110
Mahaicony River, 110
Mahdia, 104
Makus, 108
manatee, 25, **25,** 111
manganese, 16, 112

mangrove, 21
Man-Power Citizens Association
   (MPCA), 45
maps
   politics, **107**
   regional, **1**
   topographical, **2**
market, **60**, 97, **97**
Mashramani, 11, 99
Matthews Ridge, 67
Mazaruni diamond fields, 72
Mazaruni River, **12**, 19, **26**, 32,
   67, 69, 102-103, 110
Mazaruni Valley, 103
measures, 109, 119
mining, 16, 65-67, **65**, 112
missionaries, 76-77
Mittelholzer, Edgar, 87, 121
money, 109
monkeys, 24, 111
Monroe Doctrine, 56
Moore, Philip, 35, 87, 96, 121
motto, 7
mountains, 19, **19**
Mount Roraima, 19, 110
Moyne Commission, 46
Moyne, Lord, 45-46, 117
mulattoes, 79, 108
music, **4**, 88, **88**, 99, 102, 115
Muslims, 11, 80, 108
name, 13, 108
Nasser, Gamal Abdel, 96
National Assembly, 58, 108
National Cultural Center, 97, 99
National Dance Company, 88,
   115
national flower, 23
nationalization, 53
National Library, 114
National Social Insurance
   Scheme, 118
National Sports Development
   Council, 89
natural resources, 8, 16, 110, 111
Nehru, Pandit, 96
New Amsterdam, 41, 71, **100**,
   101, 109, 112, 114, 116, 117
New River, 57

newspapers, 73, 112
Nicole, Christopher, 121
Nkrumah, 96
Non-Aligned Monument, 96
Obeah practices, 81
Ocean Shark, 66-67
Ojeda, Alonso de, 30, **30**
orchids, 23, 110
Organization of American States
   (OAS), 57, 109, 119, 120
Orinduik Falls, **12**
Orinoco River, 56
Orinoco River Delta, **5**, 28
pai, 81, 113
Pakaraima Mountain, 19, **19**, 67,
   110
Palace of the Peacock (Harris), 86
Paris, Treaty of, 36
Parliament building, 94, **94**
Patamona tribe, 19
peccaries, 25, **25**, 111
People's National Congress
   (PNC), 49, 53, 73, 118
People's Progressive Party
   (PPP), 48-49, 52, 118
People's Temple, 82, 119
plant life, 21, **22**, 23, **23**, 110-111
poldering, 34, 37
political parties, 45-49
Pomeroon River, 71, 110
population, 75, 79, 109
portnocker, 66-67, 78, 104
Portuguese, 8, 41, 42, 79
Portuguese party, 51
Potaro River, **18**, 19, 110
poverty, 49
prehistoric rock paintings, **26**
president, 58, 108
Presidents College, 83, 113, 119
President's Residence, 94
prime minister, 58, 108
racial divisions, 8-9, 49, 51
radio, 73, 112
railroads, 72, 112, 117
rain forest, 7, 21, **22**, 78, 105
Raleigh, Walter, 31-32, **31**, 116
religion, 42-43, 73, 80-82, **81**, 108
Remembrance Day, 97

reptiles, 24
Reynolds Guyana Mines, 119
rice, 21, 43, **43,** 44, 49, 61, 62, **62,**
   111, 117
rivers, **12,** 15-16, **15,** 110
rock engravings, 99
Rupununi Rebellion, 118
Rupununi Savanna, 20, **20, 23,**
   64, 67, 112
Ryan, Leo, 82, 119
St. George's Cathedral, 94, **95,**
   114
saltwater grasses, 21
Sandys, Duncan, **50,** 51
savanna, 20, **20,** 21, 110
Schomburgk, Robert, 23, 56, 57,
   116
seawall, 14, **14**
1763 Monument, 96, **96**
Seymour, A. G., 121
Shahabuddeen, Mohamed, 58,
   120, 121
sharks, 24
siruaballi, 23, 110
Skeldon, 101
slaves, 8, 34-35, **34,** 39-40, 77-78,
   116
sloths, 24, **24**
social welfare, 115
society, 76, 114
sports, 88-89, **89,** 115
Springlands, 71, 101
square miles, 13, 111
Stabroek, 36, 37. *See also*
   Georgetown
Stabroek Market, 97, **97**
stingrays, 24
sugarcane, 7, 21, 33, 34, 35, **38,**
   44, 61, 63-64, **63, 64,** 111, 117
Sugar Producers' Association, 45
sugar workers strike, 46-47, **47,**
   118, 119
Suriname, 13, 14, 15, 36, 57, 71,
   110
tapir, 24, 111
telegraph service, 73
television, 73, 112
telephones, 73

Tiboku Falls, 69
Tiger Hill, 69
Tito, 96
Timehri International Airport,
   99, 112, 118
tinamou, 25
tourism, 54-55, 99, 104-105
trade, 32-33, 43, 61, 70, 113
trade unions, 44-45
transportation, 15-16, 17, 71-73,
   71, 72, 103, **103,** 112
Trinidad, 67
turtles, 24, 111
Umana Yana, 94-95, **95,** 119
unemployment, 55
United Force, 49, 52
United Kingdom, 67, 70, 72
United Nations (UN), 57-58, 109,
   118, 119
United States, 67, 70, 120
University of Guyana, 82, 113,
   118
Utashi River, 19, 110
van Hoogenheim, Governor, 35
Venezuela, 13, 14, 19, 28, 56, 57,
   70, 117, 118
Victoria, Queen, 44
Victoria Law Courts, 94
Victoria Regia lily, 23, **23,** 111,
   116
Vienna, Congress of, 36
villages, 115
vulture, 25
wallaba trees, 21, 110
Wapisianas, 76, **77**
Warrau, 27, 28, 76, **76,** 80, 108
weights, 109
West India Company, 34, 35
Williams, Aubrey, 87, 99, 121
Williams, Denis, 87, 105, 121
Wismar, 103
Woby, John Frederick, 99, 117,
   121
women, 78
Wong, Clinton, 48-49, 121
World War I, 96
World War II, 46, 96
Youman·Nabi, 11

About the Author

Marlene Targ Brill is a freelance Chicago-area writer who has published more than eighteen fiction and nonfiction books as well as produced articles, media, and other educational materials for children and adults. Ms. Brill especially enjoys writing about social studies and history topics. Among her more recent credits are *John Adams, James Buchanan*, and *I Can Be a Lawyer* for Childrens Press and *Allen Jay and the Underground Railroad* for Carolrhoda Press. She has already written *Libya, Mongolia, Algeria*, and *Guatemala* (coauthored with her brother, Professor Harry Targ) for the Enchantment of the World series.

Ms. Brill holds a B.A. in special education from the University of Illinois and an M.A. in early childhood education from Roosevelt University. She works in a home office where her husband, Richard, her daughter, Alison, and a wild poodle, Fluffy, live.